THE COMPLETE GUIDE TO GOLDENDOODLES

Erin Hotovy

LP Media Inc. Publishing

Text copyright © 2019 by LP Media Inc.

www.lpmedia.org

Publication Data

Erin, Hotovy.

The Complete Guide to Goldendoodles/ Erin Hotovy. ---- First edition.

Summary: "Successfully raising a Goldendoodle dog from puppy to old age" --- Provided by publisher.

ISBN: 978-1-09377-562-4

[1. Goldendoodles --- Non-Fiction] I. Title.

This book has been written with the published intent to provide accurate and authoritative information in regard to the subject matter included. While every reasonable precaution has been taken in preparation of this book the author and publisher expressly disclaim responsibility for any errors, omissions, or adverse effects arising from the use or application of the information contained inside. The techniques and suggestions are to be used at the reader's discretion and are not to be considered a substitute for professional veterinary care. If you suspect a medical problem with your dog, consult your veterinarian.

Design by Sorin Rădulescu

First paperback edition, 2019

Cover Photo Courtesy of Bree Wright

Oliver the Goldendoolde: @oliverthegoldendoodle on Instagram

TABLE OF CONTENTS

CHAPTER 1
Introduction to Goldendoodles

It's no secret that Goldendoodles are the hottest dog breed these days. Everywhere you look you see this fluffy, playful dog. These guys are loved for their stuffed animal–like appearance and their intelligent and playful demeanor. If you've ever spent time around a Goldendoodle, you know why their owners adore this breed. If not, this chapter will teach you about the breed that is sweeping the nation.

Photo Courtesy of Bree Wright

What Is a Goldendoodle?

Simply put, the Goldendoodle is a cross between a Golden Retriever and a Poodle. This crossbreed combines the cute and playful Golden Retriever with the intelligent and curly-coated Poodle to form a new and exciting breed. However, this cross is often more complex than mixing a Golden Retriever and a Poodle. Oftentimes, several crossbreeds are made before a lineage is available for sale.

In some cases, a Goldendoodle and a Poodle are crossed to bring out the curly coat characteristics. The more Poodle in a mix, the curlier the fur will be. This is desirable for owners who want a dog that doesn't shed very much, or just prefers the curly look. Other times, a Goldendoodle is crossed with another Goldendoodle. By crossing the same crossbreed, breeders can refine certain traits that they favor in their dogs. It takes a lot of time and expertise, but a good breeder can create a pup that has all the best traits of a Golden Retriever and all the most desired traits of a Poodle in order to make a super-dog!

Designer Dogs and Popular Pups

If you research Goldendoodles on official kennel club websites, you may find that this breed is not included. This is because many organizations do not include crossbreeds. Goldendoodles are often called "designer dogs" because they are crossbred dogs, bred to be new and exciting, with lots of desirable traits. So, while these dogs are not mutts, they are not considered purebred, no matter how good your breeder is.

Because these dogs are so popular, some breeders will even try to pass mutts off as Goldendoodles. Breeder Darren Smith of DoodlePups says it's important to check out the puppy's parents before buying a dog. To estimate the size of your pup, take the average weight of the parents. Also, check for the parents' kennel organization registration. Especially if you're unfamiliar with the breed, you don't want to pay a lot of money for a different kind of dog. It's unfortunate that dishonest breeders sell Goldendoodles to prospective owners, but it comes with the territory of buying a wildly popular dog breed.

Because designer dogs are so desirable these days, there's no shortage of breeders out there who have litters of Goldendoodles. While this makes it easier to find the dog of your dreams, it also means that there are a lot of breeders just trying to cash in on the latest trends. For this reason, you'll have to be extra careful when choosing a breeder. Later chapters will cover the ins and outs of choosing the right breeder and the right pup.

FUN FACT

Labradoodle vs. Goldendoodle

What is the difference? While Goldendoodles and Labradoodles are different mixes, these dogs can be remarkably similar. Both breeds are half Poodle. Goldendoodles are the offspring of a Poodle and a Golden Retriever, while Labradoodles come from a Poodle and Labrador. These dogs can have similar temperaments and are similar in appearance. Both dogs are also highly intelligent and make great service animals.

Photo Courtesy of
Lindsey Jones
Cheree Federico Photography

Background of Poodles and Golden Retrievers

"Both Golden Retrievers and Standard Poodles were originally bred as water retrievers. A well-bred poodle is a dignified strong dog. Since both Poodles and Goldens were bred for similar purposes, it makes sense that a Goldendoodle is a great combination."

Jennifer Tramell
Music City Goldendoodles

Because your new dog is an amalgam of two other breeds, it helps to have some information on the two parents. Crossbreeds can show any combination of traits from their parents, so it can be fun to observe your dog's appearance and behavior and try to guess where their specific traits came from.

Golden Retrievers are known for being great family pets. They were originally bred to work as hunting dogs, though many work as therapy dogs today because of their calm temperament and ability to take direction. They are energetic, obedient, and playful. These dogs can grow to anywhere between fifty and seventy-five pounds and have smooth, thick coats. Though they are calm dogs, they still need a lot of exercise and playtime to be happy and healthy. They get along great with other dogs, other people, and children. All around, this is a fantastic breed to have as a pet.

Poodles are known for their sophisticated looks and their intelligence. This breed is also fairly large, weighing anywhere between forty and seventy pounds. Of course, many owners favor the smaller versions of this breed because it's a little less dog to handle. While you may envision this breed in the show ring, they were originally bred to hunt rats. Now, they've also ventured into the companion dog territory. While images of prim and proper show dogs may lead you to believe that the Poodle is a prissy dog, this could not be further from the truth. Poodles are just as goofy and playful as any other breed. They are also very intelligent, making training a breeze.

History of the Goldendoodle

The first Goldendoodle was bred around 1970 in North America as a way to integrate the non-shedding aspect of the Poodle's coat with a Golden Retriever. This breed caught on around the nineties, as people began breeding traditional service dog breeds with Poodles, in order for blind individuals with dog allergies to obtain a service animal that didn't make them ill. However, these adorable dogs became popular with the wider public, who also wanted a version of the Golden Retriever that didn't leave fur and dander all over the house. So, while these designer dogs originally served a very specific purpose for blind people with dog allergies, they soon became available to anyone who favored the look of this fluffy crossbreed.

Photo Courtesy of Kay Patton

Physical Characteristics

Photo Courtesy of Nitin Kayathi

Goldendoodles have a distinguished look that is not unlike other Poodle crossbreeds. These are large dogs that grow to be fifty to ninety pounds, though smaller varieties don't get nearly this large. They have a wavy or curly coat, depending on their breeding. Their fur tends to be around two to three inches long, though the fur on their legs and head may be a little shorter. Most of these dogs have a gold coat, but it's also possible to have a black, white, gray, red, or brown Goldendoodle. They also have a long tail and floppy ears. These dogs have a medium build, but can get chunky if they are overfed and don't receive enough exercise. This breed should be neither bony nor stocky.

There can be a lot of variation in appearance because there isn't really a set standard for these dogs. Being a designer breed, they are not recognized by traditional kennel clubs that set these standards. Instead, they are often bred to a breeder's preference. If you like the look and temperament of the Goldendoodle, but you worry about their large stature, smaller varieties are possible. If a Golden Retriever or Goldendoodle is bred with a toy or miniature Poodle, this will result in a slightly smaller dog.

Also, the texture of the coat can vary, depending on the coat genes expressed in your pooch. The more Poodle in the dog, the curlier the coat will be. Fewer Poodle genes will result in a wavy coat. The options in coat texture allow you to choose between a cuddly teddy bear and a loveable shaggy dog. But, if you're buying this breed because of allergies, you may choose the curlier option.

Benefits of "Hypoallergenic Dogs"

The reason these dogs became so popular in the first place is because they're often referred to as hypoallergenic dogs. While there is no truly hypoallergenic dog, Poodles and Poodle crossbreeds are known for not shedding very much. This lack of a shedding coat reduces the amount of animal dander that is released into your home. This dander is part of what's responsible for the itchy eyes and runny nose that allergy suffers know too well.

However, be aware that dander is not the only matter that can trigger an allergic reaction. Saliva can also give you the allergic reaction that you're buying this breed to avoid. So, if you have severe enough allergies that you cannot own a dog without a curly coat, it's a good idea to test out a few dogs before you find one that you can be around without feeling sick. Sometimes people report an allergic response to one dog in a litter, but not another. Or, they are triggered by the saliva, and not the dander. If you're looking at a Goldendoodle because you cannot have another breed, take the time to work with a breeder and try to spend some time with the dogs so you don't end up with one that makes you sneeze.

If allergies are an issue in your home, you might find the right breeder by asking about the dogs' coats. Breeders like Beverly Eckert from Hilltop Pups will DNA test their dogs to find which ones carry specific shedding genes. That way, they can breed dogs with genes that correspond with the non-shed trait. According to this breeder, red, brown, and cream-coated poodles are more likely to produce a non-shedding coat than other colors of poodles. A breeder that goes the extra mile to ensure your new friend doesn't make you sick can be very beneficial to individuals with allergies.

Even if you don't have allergies, it can be nice to have a dog that doesn't shed all over your home. While all dogs shed a little, there is a huge difference between the amount of fur a Golden Retriever leaves behind and what a Goldendoodle gives off. If you want a dog, but aren't crazy about frequently vacuuming your floors, this breed is a good choice.

Goldendoodle Behavioral Characteristics

"Goldendoodles get their intelligence from their poodle genetics, but they also get their love, affection, and need to please from the Golden Retriever genetics, which makes them easy to train. This makes Goldendoodles one of the preferred breeds for therapy dogs."

Kristine Probst
Island Grove Pet Kennels

This breed is the epitome of human's best friend. They work well in any type of home and get along with everyone. They have a fun energy that makes them a pleasure to be around. They're silly and love to play, but they can also be calm and cuddly. This breed loves to go on long walks and play fetch for hours. They're the type that will always be eager to go outside and play, and will get bored if forced to be a couch potato.

Goldendoodles are gentle, friendly dogs that get along with everyone. If you have kids or other dogs in your family, this would be a great addition to your home. This dog is the opposite of a watch dog—Goldendoodles are known for being friendly to everyone they meet. They want to be around other people as much as possible. However, this means that they don't make a great pet for someone who is always away from the home. If left alone for too long, Goldendoodles may develop separation anxiety, which often leads to destructive habits.

Intelligence is another characteristic often seen in this breed. This intelligence will help you train your dog. These dogs love to learn new things and be challenged on a daily basis. Sometimes intelligent dogs will get bored if their minds are not kept active, so it's important to continue training and play interactive games with your Goldendoodle. A solid knowledge of commands will also keep your mischievous pup from getting into too much trouble when he makes his own rules!

Is a Goldendoodle Right for You?

After reading this chapter, you may be convinced that this is the best breed ever, but it's important to be honest with yourself before committing to a dog. Your little buddy will be attached to you from the moment you bring him home, so it's important to be confident in your ability to give him the best home he can possibly have.

First, can your home support a Goldendoodle? These are large dogs that need a lot of room to run around and may not do so well in an apartment. On the other hand, this dog thrives in a home with a fenced-in backyard. That way, there is plenty of room to roam, while ensuring your dog doesn't wander away.

Next, who's at home? This dog does just fine with other people and pets. With a little socialization, your dog will feel comfortable with anyone. But Goldendoodles do not like to be left alone. If you spend a lot of time away from home, you may need to consider a breed that can handle down time better than the Goldendoodle. This dog needs someone to keep them company.

Also, are you willing to be active? This dog thrives with the adventurous owner who loves to spend time outside. If you like to go on long walks or short jogs, then this dog will make the perfect companion. If you aren't able to meet this dog's exercise needs, there are other breeds that require a little less movement. The Goldendoodle needs plenty of opportunities to get some fresh air and get moving.

Finally, are you willing to devote your time and energy to your dog's care? This breed does best if they are well-trained and are constantly practicing their skills. This takes a lot of time and effort. Also, these dogs need to be companions, so if you're too busy or not interested in spending a lot of time with this dog, it may not be the right breed for you. With a Goldendoodle, you can plan on spending hours of your day with your dog. This is not a dog that can be left outside or passed around from home to home. When you bring this dog home, it's because you want a best friend to be by your side as much as possible.

If you answered yes to these questions, then a Goldendoodle may be a great pet for you! However, there are a lot of things you must do before you can bring your dog home; otherwise, maybe it's just a matter of waiting a few years until your home is more stable for a Goldendoodle.

Goldendoodles are unique dogs that are specifically bred to get along well in most homes. This dog is a companion animal that is certain to brighten your life. They are family-friendly dogs with coats that will help keep your house clean and keep you from sneezing. If you've decided that this dog is right for you, it's time to prepare yourself for your new friend.

CHAPTER 2
Choosing a Goldendoodle

These days, it's not too hard to find someone who's selling Goldendoodles. Their popularity means that there are more breeders selling this adorable dog. However, this also means that there are more backyard breeders and Goldendoodles in shelters than ever before. Once you decide that a Goldendoodle is right for you, it's time to figure out where to get your perfect Goldendoodle. Choosing a breeder can be a daunting process, but this chapter will give you some tips and tricks to making the buying or adopting process as smooth as possible.

Photo Courtesy of Ashley Anderson

Buying vs. Adopting

Before picking out the first available Goldendoodle, it's important to decide if you'd rather buy or adopt your dog. Both options have their pros and cons. People can be passionate about one side or the other, so it's important to ultimately do what's best for you and your household. When it comes to something as serious as picking out a new best friend for life, no one should pressure you into making a decision you would not choose without their input. It's great to consider both options so your informed choice is the best choice for you.

When buying a dog from a reputable breeder, you should have a general expectation of what your dog is going to be like. Good breeders put a lot of care and expertise into breeding the best dogs they can. This means that their pups have excellent temperaments and their coat type is compatible with owners who have dog allergies. These dogs often come with health guarantees that let you know that the dog should be free from any genetic health issues that can create devastating loss or enormous vet bills. Buying a dog from the right breeder may ensure that your dog is healthy and well-bred. Also, if you're set on showing your dog in competitions, you'll probably want a dog from champion stock.

Also, there are some benefits to bringing a puppy into your home, as opposed to a dog with previous owners. It's hard to know what commands the previous owners have taught, along with bad habits they have instilled in their dog. With a new puppy, you're the only one responsible for their behavior. Your puppy won't come with weird behaviors that have been tolerated and ignored for too long. Instead, you'll be able to correct any unwanted behaviors from an early age.

However, there are some benefits to adopting a dog. Puppies are notoriously difficult to keep up with, so an adult dog may better fit your lifestyle. Many re-homed dogs come from owners who treated their dogs well and did a good job training them. So, it's possible to welcome into your home a dog that is already potty trained and knows a few basic commands. Also, adult dogs are generally calmer than puppies and require a little less supervision and fewer bathroom breaks. In many cases, you're simply bringing a good dog into your life that someone else has already done the hard work for.

Perhaps the biggest reason people choose to adopt is because there are so many wonderful dogs out there that need a good home. Many times, the dogs in rescues and shelters are perfectly good dogs, but their owner was unable to keep them. Even if the dogs were given up for behavioral reasons, a different owner or household could turn the dog's life

Photo Courtesy of
Gabrielle Pawelko

around. Also, when more people adopt than buy, it puts puppy mills and unskilled breeders out of business. If you're interested in saving a dog's life and you're flexlble in the kind of Goldendoodle you bring into your home, then adoption is a great choice.

How to Find a Reputable Breeder

Once you decide you want to buy a Goldendoodle puppy, you'll want to find the right breeder. It's tempting to buy a dog at a discount, but these generally come from backyard breeders. In order to find the best Goldendoodle, you'll need to do some research.

First, you might want to try talking to other Goldendoodle owners. You can take recommendations for breeders and learn more about their kennels. If a dog owner had a fantastic experience with a breeder, then you might want to contact them. Ask owners questions about price, health of their pets, and ease of communication. If a fellow Goldendoodle owner raves about how great their breeder is, there's a good chance they care a lot about their business and the dogs they produce.

Your local dog organization is another great place for recommendations. A ton of networking goes on in the dog training and showing world, and if the person you contact doesn't know a breeder, there's a good chance they can put you in contact with someone who does. These people are very passionate about dogs and want to see you make the right choice when it comes to picking out a new buddy.

A veterinarian may also be able to help you find a great breeder. Vets have a large network in their community and may even work with Goldendoodle breeders. Even if they don't have names for you, they may offer tips for choosing a breeder in your area and tell you what to look out for with Goldendoodles. Anyone in your community who cares about dogs is a fantastic resource for your journey as a Goldendoodle owner.

When all else fails, a simple internet search can bring forth the kind of information you're looking for. Be careful, because even the worst breeders can create a flashy website. At the same time, a well-established breeder may not be up to date on their technology. Take the websites you find with a grain of salt. It may not be the quickest way to sort out the inexperienced breeders, but it's a start.

Researching Breeders

"Do your due diligence! Research the breeder thoroughly. Contact past buyers, their vet, their trainer, even a groomer who grooms their puppies to get info on the type of coat produced. Do not rush into a puppy purchase."

Maureen Simpson
Arizona Goldendoodles

Once you've narrowed down your selection of potential breeders, do some research to make sure they're the right one. The main thing you want to look for is some sort of proof that the breeder is in the business for the right reasons. Oftentimes, people pick up on a trend and try to capitalize on it. People with no breeding experience see that Goldendoodles are popular and want to breed their own to make money. While some of these breeders mean well and take care of their puppies, they don't necessarily have the knowledge to produce good, healthy pups. There are also breeders out there who do not treat their puppies well and are only in the breeding business to make money. These kinds of breeders should be avoided at all costs.

Photo Courtesy of
Cherrie Mahon
River Valley Doodles

A well-bred Goldendoodle puppy is not cheap. Expect to spend anywhere from $600 to $1,600 for a puppy. If you see a price that's suspiciously low, there's a good chance that there's something wrong with the dog or breeding operations. That sort of dog might still make a good companion, but you'll end up paying more in healthcare costs later on. Plus, if you have your heart set on a well-bred dog, you certainly won't be getting that for a much lower price.

You also want your breeder's dogs to have some success in the show ring, especially if you want to show your new Goldendoodle. While there is no purebred classification for Goldendoodles, puppies can still be produced by award-winning stock. Ask the breeder if their dogs or their puppies have gone on to win any awards. Also ask for details about their dogs' health. They should know which genetic illnesses are common in these breeds and be able to tell you how they avoid those illnesses in their breeding.

Finally, see if they'll let you visit their kennel. Some breeders may be hesitant to show you their dogs because they're not up to snuff. If the place where they keep the dogs is not clean, it may be safe to assume that they don't take very good care of their dogs. Since breeders generally work out of their home, it may not always be easy for a breeder to allow visitors at all hours of the day. However, a good breeder will probably be willing to spend time talking to you about their dogs, either in person or over the phone.

Health Tests, Certifications, and Contracts

As stated earlier, Goldendoodles do not have purebred designation because they are crossbreeds. However, there are still organizations that allow for crossbreeds and even set standards for appearance and behavior. The Goldendoodle Association of North America is one such club that offers membership to breeders and registers pups. Through membership, the organization supports breeders through providing learning opportunities. In return, the organization vouches for breeders. So, if your breeder is a member of a Goldendoodle organization, that means that they have spent the time and money to learn more about the breed and are working toward the set standards.

If your breeder is involved with one of these organizations, there's a good chance that they also register their pups. This means that they have a pedigree for their pup that goes back several generations. This is just another level of identification that shows you that your pup comes from good stock. The Goldendoodle organization with which your dog is registered will give you a certificate of pedigree in exchange for a fee that helps keep these breed organizations running.

Your breeder may also offer health tests and contracts. The breeder will have their dogs checked over by a vet to test for common genetic diseases. Some tests may also be done on the puppies so the breeder can sell them in good conscience. Once you buy the dog, your breeder may request that you also take the dog to your vet in the first few months, just to ensure that the dog is in good health. Later on, if your dog becomes ill, your breeder will not be responsible for it because your dog was healthy at the time of the sale. So, to protect the breeder and your new dog, you may be asked to complete a contract to have your dog checked out by a vet.

Photo Courtesy of
Ashlyn Hatfield

Photo Courtesy of
Katie Carlson

Choosing Your Pup

"Goldendoodles vary greatly in size so know what size you want and do the math despite what the breeder tells you. Combining the weight of parents and dividing by two will give you a good estimate of the dog's adult weight."

Darren Smith
DoodlePups

Once you've picked a breeder, it's time to pick a dog. Because this breed is in such high demand, it may be hard to get your pick of the litter. These days, dogs are often spoken for through the computer. After seeing a litter of adorable pups, people quickly claim them and choose by appearance. However, there's more to a good dog than just their cute looks. A dog's personality is also extremely important. Even at just a few months old, these pups start showing some character and disposition.

When it comes to choosing the best personality, it's wise to choose a personality in the middle of the pack.

For example, you don't want a dog that's too shy or too aggressive. You want a dog that's curious enough to greet you, but not so overbearing or clingy that they can't be alone. You also want to make sure that the dog is comfortable being around you and other dogs. Also, don't overlook instinct. If you have a special connection with a dog, then it's probably the right one for you!

Tips for Adopting a Goldendoodle

"If you are choosing from a rescue, consider what the pup has gone through to this point and don't expect the same pup as you would find at a breeder. Rely on the expertise of the rescue group to help you make a good decision."

Jennifer Tramell
Music City Goldendoodles

Perhaps you've decided that you'd rather adopt than buy a pup. It may be difficult to find a Goldendoodle ready for adoption when you decide you want a dog. Dogs come in and out of shelters, so you may have to wait a while for a Goldendoodle to arrive into a local shelter. In the meantime, do some research to see if there are any Goldendoodle rescues in your area. These are special shelters that are breed-specific. Volunteers will help you find the right Goldendoodle for your home because they get to know their dogs before adopting them out.

Adoption is more than paying a fee and picking up your new Goldendoodle. Because these dogs were once surrendered, the volunteers who run these shelters are very particular about the homes they go to next. Too much change can be hard on a dog, so they want their last home to be their only home for the rest of their life. With Goldendoodle rescues, you can expect a detailed application form and home visit. These organizations will want to know who lives in your home and if you have any other pets. They'll want to know where you live, what kind of experience you have with dogs, and if you have a backyard fence without any gaps for a dog to squeeze through.

Don't settle for any dog, just because they're available at the time of your search. Perhaps you had your heart set on an adult dog and the one in the shelter is a puppy. Or, maybe the dog cannot be around children and you have kids at home. It can be hard to wait for the right breed to appear in a shelter near you, but it's best not to force a dog into a situation that isn't right for it. You'll only end up with problems and will have to return the dog to the shelter. It may take a little time to find the right Goldendoodle to adopt, but it will absolutely be worth it when you're able to bring your dog to their new forever home.

HELPFUL TIP
Size Matters

Goldendoodles tend to be large-breed dogs. If you're bringing home a puppy, you may be wondering just how big it will get. If you know the height and weight of each of the puppy's parents, you can figure out approximately how big your puppy will get. Add the height or weight of each parent and divide by two to get an average estimated height or weight for your puppy when he or she grows up.

It's hard not to buy the first dog you see, but try to resist rushing into things. After all, this decision will affect the rest of your dog's life. Take your time and explore all of your options. Not only does this allow you to get the best pup for you, but you'll have time to figure out what you need to make your future dog's life as perfect as possible. Support good breeders who use ethical practices, instead of funding backyard breeding operations. Also, ask as many questions as possible. A breeder is a great source of knowledge for everything you need to know about your Goldendoodle. Learn as much as you can from them, so your dog's transition into your home is as perfect as your dog.

CHAPTER 3
Preparing Your Household for Your Goldendoodle

Before you even bring your puppy home, it's a good idea to take a few days to get your house ready for a new dog. If you wait too long, you'll find yourself scrambling to put potted plants in unreachable places while trying to wrangle an excited puppy. Preparation is key, so take some time to get ready before you bring your puppy home. Preparing for a new dog is much like baby-proofing a house—it's important to keep your dog, your other pets, and your belongings safe.

*Photo Courtesy of
Kari Bowdler*

Preparing Your Pets and Children

"Children should respect and love their new puppy. Let them have a safe place to go to away from toddlers, cats, and older dogs that may not want to be around them."

Donna LaQuiere
Music City Goldendoodles

When it comes to preparing your home, the most important things to prepare are the other living beings in your household. If you have kids and this is their first pet, they may need a primer on how to act around dogs. Similarly, if you have other pets, they will need to become acclimated to a new Goldendoodle. Later chapters will go in depth on socialization, but here are a few important things to note when bringing your dog home.

Though we often treat dogs like little people, they are still animals that will act according to their animal instincts. When your dog is interacting with kids, a responsible adult should always be supervising, especially at first. Goldendoodles are generally good with kids, but accidents happen. To prevent these, it's good to talk with kids about how to properly treat dogs.

Tell your kids that dogs can get scared if there's too much excitement. Loud noises and horseplay can send a dog into panic mode. When a dog is frightened, their first line of defense may be to separate themselves from the situation. But if they're in an enclosed area and someone is encroaching on their territory, their next defense may be to growl and bare teeth. This is a warning sign that says the dog is overwhelmed and needs some space. If this warning is ignored, the next defense is to snap or bite. This can be a devastating reaction, so teach your kids to be calm around your dog and watch for warning signs.

Also, dogs can instantly go from having fun to getting upset if they're being handled improperly. A poke in the eye or a pulled tail may startle the dog and trigger a warning reaction. Teach kids to pet a dog gently on the back and avoid the head and tail. Even a gentle, friendly dog will react when they're scared or in pain. Teach your kids that dogs can feel pain and get scared, too.

No amount of well-meaning pep talks will prepare your existing dogs or cats for a new sibling, so you'll have to try other methods of preparing

Photo Courtesy of
Nick Frega

your pets. When it comes to introducing your old pets to a new pet, you need lots of time. Never force two animals to be close. Goldendoodles are pretty good with other pets, but animals can be unpredictable. They send off many signals that are unperceivable to people, so you might not know there's an issue until there's a fight.

Take the introductory period slow. Before you even bring your dog home for good, talk to your breeder or shelter and see if you can introduce your pets in a neutral place, like a friend's house or a park. Let your pets sniff each other, but don't force them to interact. If this meeting goes well, set up another meeting in your home and see how your pets respond. If they get along well, it might be time to bring your Goldendoodle home for good!

If things don't go so well, you can keep trying. Some dogs take a while to warm up to others. However, if your meetings have gone disastrously and your older pets have been known to get along poorly with other dogs, you may want to think about whether it's a good idea to introduce a new dog into your home at this time. The last thing you want is for your dogs to fight or get injured.

Preparing Indoor Spaces

Puppies are known for putting their mouth and sharp little teeth on everything within reach. They're not doing this to be deliberatively naughty, but because they are teething and trying to figure out how their bite works. Until they learn not to chew on everything, it's best to keep all of your belongings out of reach. Otherwise, you'll come home one day to teeth marks in all of your shoes. Also, while some of your belongings won't pose much of a hazard to your dog if chewed, small objects can easily be ingested or choked on. Also, some dogs like to chew on electrical cords that can electrocute them if they chew too deeply. Especially if you plan on letting your dog roam the house, even if unattended for a few minutes, you'll want to pick up everything within reach.

Photo Courtesy of
Diane Prewitt
My Doodle Babies

Photo Courtesy of
Meghan Wilson

In the first few months of having your dog, you may want to create boundaries within your home. There are different ways to do this, depending on how much freedom you want your pup to have. To cut down on the destruction, some owners set up a pen on a hard floor to keep messes contained and wandering to a minimum. When your dog is still a little puppy, this gives them a little room to stretch their legs, while still staying contained. As your puppy grows, you may need to give them a little more space to walk around without giving them the full range of your home. A baby gate can be useful to block off sections of your home, so your dog doesn't have accidents while you're not around to supervise them. Or, you may decide to crate train your dog so they're accounted for when you're away.

Along with precautions to keep your home free of puppy destruction, it's nice to give your dog a space to feel comfortable and safe. This little part of the house can be devoted to your dog so they can hide out when they're feeling overwhelmed, or relax after an exhausting day. For some dogs, a crate serves this purpose. For others, a dog bed works well. Whichever you choose, place it in an area where people spend time so they don't feel too left out of family activities, but also in an area where no one will trip over them while they're chilling out.

Preparing Outdoor Spaces

While Goldendoodles like to spend lots of time outside, they are a companion animal that needs to spend time inside around their people. So, while your dog might spend the majority of their time inside, they will still want to have plenty of time to roam around in fresh air. A backyard is great for this breed because it allows these big dogs the freedom to run around and play in a contained environment. Fences are a must, as it ensures that your dog will stay safe on your property. Short chain-link fences may be okay when your dog is little, but as your Goldendoodle grows to become full-sized, you'll need something a little taller to keep your pooch contained. A tall, sturdy fence is great for this breed because they are so active.

If you choose to leave your dog outside for parts of the day when you are not at home, you may want to provide some sort of shelter for your Goldendoodle. In the summer, make sure you have plenty of shade and cool water for your dog. In the winter, a doghouse or even a blanket on the deck may be cozy for your dog. An outdoor umbrella or roof can provide protection from the rain. If you keep your dog outside for long periods of time, avoid tying your dog to a chain. In some situations, it might be necessary, but for general outdoor time, it's best to give your dog a little space to roam. This way, you don't have to worry about your dog getting tangled or hurting their neck if they pull too hard.

Hidden Household Dangers

HELPFUL TIP
Toxic Houseplants

Houseplants can bring color and air-cleansing properties to your home, but they can actually be toxic to your pet. While many houseplants are harmless to animals when eaten, here are some common houseplants you may want to watch out for when preparing your home for a new dog. Be aware that this is not a comprehensive list. You should check that any houseplants within your pet's reach are not poisonous to dogs.

1. Philodendron
2. Pothos
3. Peace Lily
4. Jade
5. Ivy
6. Aloe Vera

If you don't have kids or other pets in your home, you might not realize all of the dangerous things in your home, both indoors and outdoors. While there's no need to live in fear of your dog getting into something dangerous, it's good to be mindful of things your dog can get into. First, you'll want to remove any objects that your dog can choke on or get lodged in their digestive tract. A hungry puppy can gulp down spare change, washcloths, and even dog toys that are ripped beyond recognition.

Next, be mindful of the chemicals you keep around the house. While it probably wasn't a big deal to keep air fresheners on the coffee table, cleaning products on the laundry room floor, and the toilet seat up before getting a dog, it is now. You'd be amazed at how crafty dogs can be when they're trying to get a forbidden treat. You may start closing the bathroom and laundry room doors to keep your pup out, and set your air fresheners on a higher shelf. Even foods like candy that once sat in bowls on the counter will need to be moved to a cupboard. Also, many lawn and pesticide products can be deadly to dogs, so do a quick cleanup of your shed and garage while you're at it.

Finally, you may want to examine your houseplants and landscaping. There are a lot of plants that can make a dog sick if they ingest them. Common outdoor plants like hostas, ivy, and lilies can make a dog ill. Do a little research on the plants in your home and garden to see if they are dog-friendly. This doesn't necessarily mean that you need to dig up your yard, but if your dog has a tendency to munch on plants, keep an eye on the ones they find delicious, and plant dog-safe ones in the future.

With a little work, your home can be a comfortable and welcoming place for a new Goldendoodle. The most important thing you can do is to make sure there are no dangers in your home. This includes children, pets, and common household items. Also, it's necessary to prevent your new dog from destroying all of your belongings. Because puppies can't control their urge to chew, it's best to keep all of your belongings out of reach until they learn what they're allowed to chew and what they aren't. Finally, give your dog their own little nook for relaxation. Dogs love to have their cozy, little dens, so choose a soft place for your dog to hang out. If you complete these steps before your dog even comes home, you'll have more time to cuddle and play, and less time to feel stressed about all of the big changes.

CHAPTER 4
Bringing Your Goldendoodle Home

"Accept the Murphy Goldendoodle Law: if a puppy can get into trouble, chew something, or potty somewhere - they will."

Jennifer Tramell
Music City Goldendoodles

Once you find the right breeder, pick a pup, and get your home squared away, it's finally time to bring your new Goldendoodle home! This is a very exciting time for your household, but it can also be somewhat stressful. New puppies require a lot of care and attention. There's so much to do, but this chapter will guide you through a few tasks you'll want to complete before your dog comes home, and within the first few weeks.

Planning for Your Goldendoodle

As mentioned in earlier chapters, ample preparation for your new Goldendoodle will make all the difference between a happy homecoming and a stressful start to your dog's new life. It is much easier to organize your home without a ball of energy running around. Then, once you have your puppy, you can spend more time having fun and training, and not worrying about rounding up supplies or finding a veterinarian.

The Goldendoodle is a sensitive dog. This makes them a fantastic companion and therapy animal, because they are so in tune with people's emotions. However, this also means that they can react according to your emotions. For example, if you're calm in a tense situation, they'll look to you and follow your lead. If you're stressed out and wound up, they may also display signs of anxiety. So, for the good of your home, prepare a little in the early days so you and your dog will stay cool.

The First Night at Home

After a long day of smelling all of the new scents and playing with all of their new friends, your Goldendoodle will probably be pretty tired. However, the first night can be scary for a new puppy. Your Goldendoodle is used to sleeping beside his mother and siblings in a familiar house. Your home smells different from what they know and they might not be so sure about their new humans. At night, it's dark and quiet and your puppy is bound to get lonely. Pair that with a tiny bladder that needs to be emptied every few hours, and you've got a whiny puppy on your hands. This is totally normal and your dog's bedtime routine will get easier as time goes on. However, the first night (and the first few weeks) might be a bit of a struggle. To help comfort your dog, Dede Hard of Red Cedar Farms recommends you bring a small towel to rub on the littermates to pick up a familiar scent. Then, put the towel in the crate at night so your dog can feel like they're with their littermates again.

To lessen your dog's anxiety, make sure they are exhausted by the time you go to bed. Give them plenty of play and exercise in the hours leading up to bedtime. Hopefully, they'll be so tired they'll fall right asleep. Also, it's important to take your dog out right before bed. That way, they won't start crying twenty minutes later because they have to go.

Not all owners want to teach their dog to sleep in their bed. While a tiny puppy doesn't take up a ton of space, a fully grown Goldendoodle does. When you instill these habits in a pup, it's hard to change your policies when your dog is big. If you don't want your dog on your bed, re-

Photo Courtesy of Brianna Scott

strain from letting your puppy hop up on the bed. Besides, puppies are known to have accidents, and you don't want to have to change your sheets every day!

Instead, place your dog's bed or crate near your room. That way, they can see and smell you, without having to be in your personal space. The proximity will also allow you to know when your dog wakes up and needs to go outside. As your dog becomes more comfortable in your home, you can move the bed or crate back to a more suitable location. You don't want your dog to learn that they can disrupt your sleep, so try to get them to sleep on their own as soon as possible.

Choosing a Veterinarian

If you don't already have a vet, this is the time to find one. A good veterinarian is your go-to person for everything concerning the health and well-being of your Goldendoodle. If you live in a town where there are multiple vet clinics, you'll have to choose the right one for you. This may be as simple as going to your nearest clinic, but not all veterinary offices are created equal. So, you may have to make some choices regarding your dog's care.

A referral from a friend or breeder can be useful. Since you'll be spending time with the person in charge of your dog's healthcare, you'll want to choose a person you like and trust. It's also advantageous to see a vet that works with Goldendoodles, like your breeder's vet, so they have Goldendoodle health concerns at the forefront of their mind.

Veterinarian clinics can differ from facility to facility. Some are just basic clinics with a vet who can diagnose issues and prescribe medication. Others have a laboratory where blood and stool samples can be analyzed to check for various conditions. Larger clinics have surgery units or emergency services. So, you need to decide what kinds of services you want your vet clinic to have. If you choose a vet without emergency services, it's a good idea to have the contact information for an emergency vet readily available. You never know when you'll need to rush your dog to the vet and you don't want to be doing research for the first time when something happens.

Before your first visit to the vet, do your veterinarian a favor and prepare your dog for the examination. This can be done by getting your dog used to being touched on the snout, ears, and belly. A puppy might be confused as to why a stranger is touching them in a strange way, but if you practice with them, they will be more likely to stay still during an exam than if it's totally foreign to them.

Supplies to Have Ready

"The most important thing to have ready is a crate. This will not only aid in house breaking but will keep the puppy safe when it can't be watched over. The crate also provides a personal space for the puppy to have alone time."

Maureen Simpson
Arizona Goldendoodles

Before your Goldendoodle comes home, you should have some supplies on hand so you don't have to leave your dog at home alone to go shopping. It may seem like you're spending a lot of money all at once, but some of these supplies will last you the entirety of your dog's life.

First, you'll need a sturdy collar and leash. A flat, buckled collar is good for everyday use. You'll want something that fits snugly, but is comfortable for your dog to wear every day. On this collar, you'll want to put an identification tag on the front loop, in case your dog gets lost and needs to be identified. These can be etched onto a tag of your choice at the pet store. You'll also need a four- or six-foot leash. A four-foot

Photo Courtesy of
Alina Bina

leash might be more comfortable for you at the beginning because you'll want to teach your dog to walk close to your side. Retractable leashes are popular, but they make it hard to control your dog. A strong nylon leash that can withstand your dog's strength is perfect. A Goldendoodle is a big, strong dog, and you want a collar and leash that can withstand a little pulling if your dog suddenly lunges for a squirrel while on a walk.

Next, you'll need dishes, food, and treats. A good puppy formula is important for giving your Goldendoodle the nutrients they need to grow into healthy adults. Then, you'll switch to an adult formula as your dog reaches full size. Later chapters will cover food and nutrition in more detail. Treats are important to have at all times. If you want to train your dog to do anything, you'll need to have some tasty treats.

HELPFUL TIP
Buying a Bed

Next, you'll need grooming supplies. A Goldendoodle's fur needs to be brushed regularly to keep from getting matted. Because they don't shed a lot of fur and have a single coat, a basic pin brush should be enough to keep your dog tangle-free and shiny. It might also be a good idea to keep a bot-

When buying a dog bed for your new Goldendoodle, there are number of things to consider. Even though your puppy may be small now, Goldendoodles are typically considered a large-breed dog. One option is to buy a dog bed that you believe your puppy won't outgrow. Another option is to buy a cheaper bed for the first six months of your dog's life and then upgrade to a nicer bed once your puppy has reached his or her full size.

tle of dog shampoo on hand in case your pup gets into something dirty or stinky. If you plan on cutting your dog's toenails, a good set of clippers will come in handy. Find a pair that cuts the nail instead of crushing it. Some clippers even come with a guard that prevents you from cutting too much of the nail off if your dog gets squirmy. A toothbrush and toothpaste are also necessary for your dog's oral health. Pet stores sell brushes that are specially designed to fit a dog's mouth and come with toothpastes with dog-friendly flavors like poultry or peanut butter.

Toys and chews are also important for Goldendoodles. Goldendoodles are extremely playful and active. A variety of sturdy toys can keep their interest for hours, preventing them from acting out from boredom. A good selection of toys will make your best friend very happy and keep them occupied. Choose a toy that's fun to chase around the yard, like a ball or a Frisbee, something that is interactive, like a tug rope, something that works their mind, like a food puzzle, and something that gives into their animal instinct, like a squeaky toy. These basics will keep your dog from getting tired of the same old games every day. You can even keep these toys on rotation so their old toys feel fresh and new to them.

It's also necessary for your dog to have something to chew. Otherwise, they will bite everything you own. It's only natural for dogs, especially puppies, to chew. It calms them down and keeps their mind busy. Teething puppies need to chew because it helps them work their new teeth through their gums. Choose a size-appropriate chew toy that cannot break or splinter into small pieces that can be choked on. Pet stores sell different types of real and synthetic bones and animal materials to keep your dog busy.

Photo Courtesy of
Kristina Snellen

Finally, you'll need a crate, a bed, or both for your dog's relaxation and security. A soft dog bed is a good place for your dog to chill out while she's hanging out the family. Find one that's the right size for your Goldendoodle, and make sure it has plenty of padding. Crates also make excellent sleeping spots. When it comes to picking the right size, choose one large enough for your dog to turn around in circles in, but not so big that they can roam around. It should be like a cozy den, not a small room.

How Much Will This Cost?

Pet supplies can add up very quickly. When you start to factor how much your dog is going to cost you, it seems like a budget-breaker. For this reason, it's important to set aside a budget for your new pet. Barring any medical complications, the first year of their life will probably be the most expensive for you. You'll have to buy all new supplies and make frequent visits to the vet for checkups and shots. Once you learn your Goldendoodle's preferences, you'll be able to buy foods and treats in bulk, and you won't waste your time buying toys and chews your dog doesn't play with.

Prices for supplies and services varies from place to place, so it's difficult to come up with an accurate prediction for every owner. Also, it makes a huge difference in budget if you buy a super expensive dog food compared to a bargain brand one. This estimation of how much your Goldendoodle will cost in the first year of his life should be used as a guide to give you an idea of how much you may need to spend. Of course, location and choices make a big difference in cost, but hopefully, you'll start to figure out how to budget for your pup.

First of all, to buy a Goldendoodle from a good breeder, you will likely spend anywhere from $600 to $1,600. If you choose to adopt, that's somewhere around $100 to $200, which includes spay/neuter surgery, shots, and microchipping. If you buy your dog, a spay/neuter surgery is on average around $75. If you want a Goldendoodle but can't afford to spend thousands on the dog, adoption is the way to go.

Yearly veterinary costs will be around $200 to $500 for basic services. Not all vaccines are required on a yearly basis, so some visits will cost more than others. You'll also need to budget at least a hundred dollars on heartworm medication and flea and tick preventative. Basic veterinary care is non-negotiable when it comes to the well-being of your dog. Even a perfectly healthy dog needs preventative care.

Photo Courtesy of
Kayla Edds

Next, you'll have to buy a lot of dog food during the course of a year. The average dog eats about $400 worth of dog food per year. Depending on which size of Goldendoodle you get, you may get away with spending less than average. So, if you're purchasing a Miniature Goldendoodle, you'll save a little on dog food. You'll also need lots of treats for training purposes, which will cost you about a hundred dollars a year. You don't necessarily need to buy expensive treats, but you'll need something that your dog likes enough to perform commands for.

Then, there are all of the supplies you'll buy right away. Leashes, grooming equipment, and dishes will add up. You'll also need some fun toys and chews for your dog. In total, you're looking at spending around two hundred dollars around the time you bring your dog home. Hopefully, some of these are one-time costs. You may want to even buy higher-quality items so you won't have to replace them later on.

It's hard to estimate how much your dog will cost you, but you could spend around a thousand dollars the first year, not including the dog. Over a dog's lifetime, it's said that the average person spends around $10,000 on their pup. This seems like a lot of money now, but once you get your dog adjusted into their new home, you'd spend all of your money to make your dog happy. If you feel as though you can't possibly come up with the funds to raise a dog, maybe wait a while until your finances are more secure. Or, you can even foster a Goldendoodle for a little while. In the end, owning a Goldendoodle is absolutely worth the cost, even though it can seem overwhelmingly expensive when it's all put down on paper.

Puppy Classes

During the first few months, it's good to get your Goldendoodle puppy enrolled in a puppy training class. Not only is this a good way to teach the basics of obedience to your little pup, but it's great for socializing your dog with other pups and their owners. They may not accomplish much more than the sit and down command during these classes, but they will teach your dog how to respond and work with you.

This may be the first time your dog has interacted with others. Socialization is so important at this age. Give your dog plenty of opportunities to sniff out the other dogs and accept pets from people. Classes are generally pretty small, so it shouldn't be too overwhelming for your puppy.

Also, training classes are a great way to interact with dog trainers. Dog trainers are another resource that you'll want to keep in contact with through the life of your dog. Whenever you're faced with a behavioral problem, you can go to your trainer for advice, because they know your dog and have worked with them before. Training classes are less about training your dog and perhaps more about training the owner. In these classes, you'll learn the basics of dog training, which will provide you with the skills you need to train your dog at home.

The first few weeks of owning a dog can be overwhelming with all of the things to buy and all of the things to do, but remember to take time to enjoy the early days. It's so much fun to have a tiny puppy, so don't get so stressed out that you forget to have fun. There are a lot of expenses associated with raising a dog, but if you stick to your budget, it shouldn't be a problem. Again, if you prepare as much as possible for your new dog, you won't feel stressed about all of the new, exciting changes.

CHAPTER 5
Puppy Parenting

Owning a puppy is so much fun! You'll enjoy taking your puppy places and showing everyone how cute he is. You'll also take a million pictures and play all day long. While having a puppy is great, it's also a lot of work. The first few months will be full of trips outside, accidents inside, and chewed-up belongings. This is the period of time when your dog is learning how to be a pet. It takes a ton of work and patience, but eventually, your Goldendoodle will learn how to be a member of your family. This chapter will guide you through some of the struggles you might face in the puppy stage, and how to get through them.

Photo Courtesy of
April Power
Power Puppies LLC

Standing By Your Expectations

If you've never owned a dog before, you might not have set rules and expectations for your pup. Or, you have a good idea of how you want your dog to behave in your home. When raising a new dog, it's important to set some behavioral expectations and stand by them. Otherwise, your dog will become confused and not know how to behave.

STORY
Dogs of Instagram

In the age of social media, many people create accounts for their dogs in order to share all of the adorable photos they capture of their furry companions. One Goldendoodle in particular, Oliver of North Carolina, has 52,000 followers on popular photo-sharing platform Instagram. Oliver lives with his owner, Breanna Wright, who dresses him up in a variety of festive costumes throughout the year. You can follow his adventures on Instagram @ oliverthegoldendoodle.

For example, you may decide that you will not allow your dog to sit on the furniture in your house. This is perfectly reasonable, as dogs often track dirt onto beds and couches. If you set this rule, you must stick by it and correct your dog every time they try to jump on your bed. If you decide to let your dog sleep with you when your partner is gone, but you scold your dog for jumping on the bed during the day, your dog will likely become confused. Dogs don't understand conditions and will not understand why they can go on the bed some nights and not others.

Or, perhaps you've decided that you will not tolerate barking in your home. If this is your rule, you must correct your dog if they bark, every single time. If you're not in the mood to correct your dog one day and just pop some earplugs in your ears, your dog may learn that they can now get away with barking, making it harder to correct in the future.

It's perfectly reasonable for your expectations to change once you get a feel for how life with your dog is going to go. Like if you originally didn't want your dog to sit on your couch, but you later decided that you want to cuddle with your dog at night, that's perfectly fine, as long as you don't change your mind again and confuse your pup.

Your entire household should follow these same rules or the training won't be as effective. Once you've decided that you don't want your dog to beg at the table for scraps of people food, your efforts will be undermined by a family member slipping scraps to your dog. Have a talk with your family or roommates about which behaviors are desired and which are not when it comes to your dog.

How to Crate Train

Crate training is an excellent tool to have in your repertoire. A crate should not be thought of as a doggy holding cell, but a cozy nook for your dog to hang out in. A crate makes a good sleeping spot, as well as a hiding place when things are getting a little too hectic. For a new puppy, a crate is a good place to hang out for short periods of time when no one is around to supervise. Because the dog is contained, they cannot make messes all over the house.

Photo Courtesy of Kaylea Garmon

However, the crate should never be used for punishment. A dog will develop an aversion to the crate if they feel scared or upset while being forced in the little space. This will also defeat the purpose of using the crate as a safe space for your dog to cool down when they get overwhelmed. Also, the crate should not be used for long stretches of time. Goldendoodles need some room to roam around and should not be kept in a crate for the entirety of your work day. Leaving them alone for too long will cause them to associate the crate with negative feelings.

Your puppy may not naturally want to crawl into the crate, so you'll have to slowly acclimate them to their new little den. Don't force your dog inside, but let them wander in with a little help. Place a tasty treat inside and let them wander inside on their own time. Eventually, they'll get curious and grab the treat. Give your dog praise if they reach inside for the treat.

Over time, raise the stakes. Take a treat and place it further back in the crate so they have to go all the way inside to get the reward. After a few times, close the front gate for a second and give them a treat if they stay calm. Then, leave the crate closed for a little bit longer. You can even put food and water dishes inside so your dog has to venture in to eat and drink. The goal is to get to the point where your dog is comfortable being in the crate for a long car ride or a night of sleep.

Chewing

"Pick up anything you do not wish the new puppy to chew on. All puppies are teething and have the need to chew. Provide them with toys that are meant for a teething puppy."

Kristine Probst
Island Grove Pet Kennels

If this is your first puppy, you will soon learn that they love to put their teeth on everything. Dogs chew because it keeps them calm and entertained, plus, it's good for their teeth. Puppies chew even more because they're trying to get their adult teeth to poke through their gums and it can be uncomfortable. The chewing helps with the teething process, and your dog does not care what they need to gnaw on to aid the process.

In order to prevent your belongings from being destroyed, you must supply your pet with acceptable chewing items. It is unfair to scold your

dog for chewing on your furniture, but not supply a suitable alternative. Your dog may have some trouble distinguishing appropriate and forbidden chews at first, but with your guidance, they will learn to know the difference.

Supply your puppy with a variety of toys that are fun to gnaw on. A sturdy bone, natural or nylon, is a good place to start. Rawhides and antlers are also fun for dogs. However, if your dog is gulping an entire rawhide bone down in one sitting, you might want to find something sturdier, or your dog may get an upset stomach. Watch out for bones that splinter easily, because the sharp pieces can hurt your dog's digestive tract when swallowed. If your dog seems to be more interested in your shoes than a dog bone, try one that is filled or flavored. Your dog might need a little extra incentive to chew.

If your dog can't be redirected to a suitable alternative to your belongings, you'll have to create aversions to their favorite objects to nibble on. Pet stores sell sprays that are non-toxic, but taste bad to dogs. You can mist the heels of your shoes or table legs to keep your dog from chewing. Also, you can clap your hands when your dog is in the act and move them to an area of the house with chew toys. When they pick up a bone, give them a reward and some praise.

Growling and Barking

Puppies love to interact with people, and sometimes this interaction is vocal. It's not reasonable to expect Goldendoodles to stay silent all the time, but it's fine to want some peace and quiet every once in a while. Barking usually happens because your dog is stimulated by something, or they want your attention. Unfortunately, you cannot always give them what they want. Giving them cuddles every time they bark for attention will only enforce that behavior. So, it's important to praise and reward your dog when they are quiet and calm.

Growling is different from barking. Growling means that your dog is upset and needs some space to calm down. This may be rare in the friendly Goldendoodle, but it's something to watch out for, especially when your dog is around young children or other pets. If your dog is growling, lead them to a quiet area, or have everyone back up so your dog can calm down.

Photo Courtesy of
Bev Eckert
Hilltop Pups

Biting

Because puppies are learning how to use their mouths, they tend to bite everything, including people. If your dog bites you, it's not because they're trying to hurt you. Instead, they're just trying to figure you out. When dogs play, they often bite down on their playmates. Again, this is not a malicious act, but a playful act. However, puppies do not know how hard they can bite before causing pain. Other dogs teach them by yelping when the puppy has caused them pain. The puppy takes this feedback and will bite a little softer next time they play.

But, because you don't want your Goldendoodle to bite anyone, you must teach them that they cannot bite you at all. Instead of scolding your dog when they nibble on your fingers, let out a high-pitched yelp, and watch your dog's mouth release instantly. They will know that they did something wrong. If you yelp every time your dog puts their mouth on you, no matter how gently, they will eventually stop the act altogether. Your Goldendoodle will think you're the most delicate dog ever and be a little gentler with you than they are with their dog buddies.

Separation Anxiety

Goldendoodles are companion animals and they love to be around their people at all times. It's normal for your dog to be a little disappointed when you're not around, and thrilled when you're home. However, separation anxiety is a condition where your dog cannot handle being alone and suffers great distress because of it. This distress may cause your dog to become destructive.

Excessive stress is not good for your dog's body, nor is it good for your household if your dog has accidents or shreds your couch because of it. If the anxiety is severe enough, your vet may need to prescribe medication. However, vets generally don't like to medicate dogs for long periods of time, unless there is no other option. Luckily, there are a few things you can try to help ease your dog's distress.

First, stop making a big deal out of entering and exiting the house. All owners like when their dog is overjoyed to see them at the end of the day, so it's natural to add extra emphasis to this action to get the desired reaction. And, sometimes it's hard to leave your best friend without lots of pets and baby talk. However, drawing attention to your absence makes your dog feel like they need to pay attention to it. Instead, leave your house without saying a word, and return quietly and give your dog a simple pat on the head when they greet you. Practice coming and go-

Photo Courtesy of Gabrielle Pawelko

ing so your dog gets used to people leaving him alone for short periods of time.

Also, give your dog as much exercise as possible. Tired dogs are good dogs because they aren't filled with energy. If your dog has too much energy and a reason to freak out, they will make activities to burn that anxious energy. If you take your dog on a walk before you leave, they may just nap while you're gone. Another way to burn mental energy is by giving your dog a puzzle toy to occupy their time. These puzzles can be filled with treats so they stay interested. Perhaps instead of pouring your dog's breakfast into a bowl, you can put it in a puzzle ball and let them work for every piece of kibble. A food-driven dog can stay occupied with these toys as long as the food is around.

If you can't troubleshoot this issue, talk to a vet or a trainer for ideas. They may notice a problem you never thought of. Or, they can teach you training skills that can help relieve anxiety in your pup. Of course, practice staying calm around your dog. Sensitive dogs like the Goldendoodle look to their owner for non-verbal cues on how to act. If you show your dog that there's nothing to worry about, they'll be more likely to settle down.

Leaving Your Puppy Home Alone

Let's face it—it's hard to have a puppy and a full-time job that keeps you away from the house for hours at a time. While adult dogs can go a few hours without needing to go potty, a little puppy can hold it for an hour, at best. Your puppy will have accidents while you're at home, so you can only imagine the mess a puppy can make when it's home alone for hours at a time. So, before you bring your dog home, work out a plan for taking care of your dog until you can trust him to be home alone.

Crates are effective for a few hours at a time, but your dog may be distressed if they're caged up for too long. If you are crating your dog while you're home, make sure you can come home at lunch and give your puppy lots of exercise. The same goes for any type of playpen you may use.

As you'll find in the next chapter, housetraining will really mess with your regular schedule. Stay flexible and use your resources. You may end up spending a little more money on your dog to make sure they go out when they need to, but it's worth it when your dog is happy and entertained.

Puppies are so much fun to have around, especially fluffy little Goldendoodle puppies. However, they are a ton of work to manage and will test your patience at every turn. Stay calm, because your puppy looks to you for how to act in your home. It's important to give your dog lots of exercise and attention in this first year, so they don't destroy your home and drive you nuts. Enjoy the hectic fun while it lasts, because your Goldendoodle will soon be a big dog that you can't scoop off of the ground and cuddle. Of course, your adult Goldendoodle will be just as cuddly as his puppy self, just much bigger!

Photo Courtesy of
LeeAnn Gott

CHAPTER 6
Housetraining

"They take far longer to potty train than you would expect. It will happen, don't lose patience and keep your expectations low."

Cherrie Mahon
River Valley Doodles

Housetraining is perhaps the most difficult part of owning a puppy. Tiny dogs have tiny bladders, so they need to go outside frequently. As a rule of thumb, dogs can hold it for as many hours as months they are old. So, a three-month-old dog can go three hours between bathroom breaks before they're absolutely bursting. However, a meal or a drink can throw off the schedule, so you should probably take your dog outside at least every hour until you get to know your dog's routine.

Different Options for Potty Training

While taking your dog to a nice, grassy spot to do their business is the norm, there are alternatives you can use to make life easier. Especially if you live in an apartment or a house without a backyard, you may need a little help. Some owners line a pen or crate with newspaper to keep messes at bay because it's disposable, but newspaper isn't very absorbent and your dog may not make it to the newspaper before they have an accident.

If you know your dog is going to have accidents inside and you're okay with this, you may want to purchase some type of disposable potty mat for your dog. Puppy pads are popular because they're absorbent, disposable, and contain enzymes that make your dog want to potty on the pad, and not the exposed floor. That way, you can control where your dog goes to the bathroom inside. There will still be a smell, but as long as you clean up quickly, it won't be a huge issue. The downside to these pads is that it creates a lot of waste, they're expensive, and it encourages your dog to use the house as a toilet. There are also products that look like fake grass that serve the same purpose, but are meant to be rinsed and reused. This product is closer to the outdoor potty, but is a hassle to clean up. These potty products may be helpful in a pinch, but are not great long-term solutions.

The First Few Weeks

Prepare to go outside on a frequent basis during these first few weeks of your puppy's life in your home. In fact, prepare to go out more than your dog actually needs to go out. Even if your dog doesn't potty when they're outside, you're reducing the risk of a later accident. It may feel like overkill, but you're helping your dog learn that they cannot use your home as a toilet.

Try to go to the same spot outside every time you go out. Dogs use the scent from their poop and pee to find a place to squat or lift a leg. When they find these scent markers, it tells them to go in that location—that's what makes puppy pads so effective. Not only does having a potty corner of the yard make it easier for them to go, but also it makes it much easier for you to clean up after. Also, if your dog has a potty corner, you're less likely to wander into their mess later on.

Make sure to go out shortly after meals. There's a good chance your dog will have to go about thirty minutes after eating. You also need to go out first thing in the morning and right before bed. Of course, you will

HELPFUL TIP
Consistency is Key

Goldendoodles are very intelligent dogs and are often quick to pick up on new tricks. Because of this, it's important to remain consistent with your expectations and follow a routine while house-training your new dog. Your puppy may benefit from a rigid eating schedule that coincides with a house-training schedule. Using a consistent verbal command when taking your puppy to his designated bathroom area will also help your Goldendoodle learn this new trick in no time.

also probably have to go out in the middle of the night or clean up accidents in the morning.

When it comes to cleaning up accidents, you must be thorough, or else your dog will find the scent and use that spot again. You might not be able to smell the mess, but your dog can. Pet stores sell enzymatic cleansers that remove that scent marker that gives them the urge to go.

Eventually, your little pup will be a big dog that can hold it for hours at a time. Until then, make sure you're giving your dog plenty of opportunities to go outside, instead of having accidents in your house.

Rewarding Positive Behavior

Dogs learn new things by receiving positive reinforcements when they do something right. In terms of housetraining, you must give them a reward every time they go to the bathroom outside. This can be in the form of praise, a treat, or both. When enforcing any behavior, you want your dog to be thrilled with the reward. So, when your dog goes to the bathroom outside, make sure they feel loved and excited so they have some incentive to go outside again.

Never punish a dog for having an accident in the house. Dogs do not learn through negative reinforcement very well and you'll end up doing more harm than good. Berating or swatting at your dog for having an accident will only make them afraid of you. Also, when it comes to training your dog to go to the bathroom outside, you can't correct your dog for an accident if you don't witness it and correct it on the spot.

For example, a lot of people think that if you rub a dog's nose in their excrement and yell at them, they are teaching their dog not to have accidents in the house. Instead, they are frightening and confusing their dog. Dogs do not have a memory that allows them to connect a past event, like pooping on the floor, and the action of an angry owner making them

Photo Courtesy of
Pam McCoy

smell it. They will be utterly confused and upset that you're mad at them for no reason. If this owner behavior continues, the dog may avoid the anger by pooping in places where the owner can't find it immediately, saving them from being in trouble. They may also be hesitant to go to the bathroom outside because they think you'll get mad at them. If you catch your dog in the act of having an accident, try to get him outside as quickly as possible and praise him for a completed job. If he doesn't make it, don't draw any attention to the mess.

It can be frustrating if you're housetraining your dog and they're slow to pick up on what you want them to do. However, it's essential that you remain positive and keep trying to find teaching moments. Remember, if your dog has an accident inside, simply clean it up and move on. The real learning happens outside when your dog does exactly what you want him to do. Give tons and treats and praise and stay positive.

Crate Training, Playpens, and Doggy Doors

"Crates should be small or have a divider for sleeping. They should be no larger than the puppy can get up and turn around in at first. Most pups will not potty in their den space. But they may potty in the corner, away from sleep space, if the crate is too large."

Tamara Spridgeon
Daizy Doodles

Photo Courtesy of Cassie Weaver

Keeping your dog in an enclosed space may help you with housetraining. Dogs like to have dens, and they like to keep them clean. That means that your dog is less likely to soil their living quarters if they're cozy, as opposed to spacious. A dog that sleeps in a crate may be more likely to notify you with a whine when they need to go, instead of leaving a mess for you to find later. A crate or pen can also keep messes in one space for you to easily clean up.

If you have a fenced-in yard, a doggy door might be an option for housetraining if you're not home enough to prevent accidents. This little flap in your back door allows your dog to come and go as he pleases, so he can go outside when nature calls. There are a few downfalls to letting your dog act upon his personal whims. For starters, your dog can take anything from inside the house into your backyard. Also, outdoor things (and creatures) can get inside. While a doggy door is an option for housetraining, be aware of the negative aspects of opening the outside to your dog.

Hiring Extra Help

Unless you work from home, it's hard to give a puppy the attention they need during the housetraining stage. Because of this, many dog owners resort to locking their dog in small spaces for too many hours, or let their dog use the bathroom inside, detracting from the housetraining practice. There are so many resources out there for dog owners to use that will make their life so much easier.

A doggy daycare is a place where you can send your dog to interact with other dogs and get the supervision they need. These places have trained staff that will clean up after your puppy as your Goldendoodle makes new friends. As an added bonus, your pup will get a ton of exercise and interaction with others, which will make them exhausted by the time you pick them up.

Dog walkers can also help you with the housetraining process by coming to your house around the time your dog needs to be let out. For example, if you can't go home for your dog's mid-morning potty break, hire a dog walker to come to your house and take your dog on a short stroll. This way, your dog gets a little more practice going outside and can stretch their legs. These days, hiring a dog walker is as simple as using a phone app. Some apps will tell you when your dog walker arrives at your house and when they leave, along with any important information about the walk.

Before you know it, your Goldendoodle will be housetrained and you won't have to worry about accidents in your home ever again. Until then, remember to stay positive and give your dog lots of rewards for a job well done. Never punish your dog for an accident. If your dog has an accident, do a good job cleaning it up and try to watch them a little closer next time so you can catch your dog's warning signs that they need to go outside. Goldendoodles are fast learners, but they need you to steer them in the right direction. It takes a lot of work and attention to housetrain a dog, but it's such an important part of raising a puppy.

CHAPTER 7
Socializing with People and Animals

Once your Goldendoodle is home, you may be so in love with your new friend that you never want to leave the house again. However, there will be a time when you want to take your dog out into the world. There, you'll encounter strange people and new dogs. If you want your dog to respond positively to new people, socialization is a must.

The Importance of Good Socialization Skills

"At first, try to ensure positive meetings by introducing your pup to animals that you know are friendly. As your pup gets older, let them meet as many other animals as they want. Pretty soon, seeing another animal will be no big deal."

Darren Smith
DoodlePups

Imagine you're at the dog park, trying to burn some of your dog's energy. Your Goldendoodle has been bouncing off the walls and you need him to settle down for a few hours so you can get work done around the house. But, when you get to the park, your dog cowers in the corner, refusing to interact with the other dogs or people, and eventually runs to the gate, begging to go home. Having burned no energy playing at the park, your dog is demanding of your time and you get nothing done at home. This is a frustrating situation that could have been prevented with more socialization at a young age.

If your dog never interacts with others, then they won't learn how. Just as with humans, dogs need to practice being social. Otherwise, they will act inappropriately and feel uncomfortable in social settings. This education in how to be social should be early on in a dog's life, between four and eight months. If you've adopted an adult dog that has social problems, it's still possible to socialize your dog. However, it will be more challenging as your adult dog has left that crucial time window.

Once you have your dog, you'll want to take him everywhere. However, if he can't get along with others, you're putting both your dog and

other people at risk. A poorly socialized dog may get so stressed out that they create further aversions to others and act out in fear. Good socialization and good breeding should result in a calm, happy Goldendoodle who just wants to be friends with everyone.

Behavior Around Other Dogs

"Wait until the puppy has ALL their shots before meeting any other dogs. Even though the other dogs may have all their shots they can still carry diseases to your puppy."

Maureen Simpson
Arizona Goldendoodles

Goldendoodles are generally friendly with other dogs. However, if your dog has a few bad experiences with other dogs, then that can cause your dog to be nervous around his peers. Ideally, you want your dog to be able to play with others without becoming too aggressive or too passive. You don't want your dog to be the one that lashes out at other dogs, nor cowers in fear at the sight of another pooch.

To teach your dog how to get along with other dogs, you'll want to start slow and not push your dog into socialization. Try visiting someone with a friendly dog for a play date. Your dogs can play with supervision and limited factors that might cause a dog stress. If your dog handles this interaction well, try a larger group of dogs, like a puppy training class. These classes are still relatively small, so your dog can become accustomed to practicing commands around a few others. Finally, try going to a dog park, where dogs of all ages and sizes can interact.

During these interactions, try to stay calm and don't be a helicopter owner. It's easy to get worried when your growing Goldendoodle is being nipped by a German Shepherd, but as long as no one is getting hurt, your dog will be okay. Jumping in to rescue your dog from what you might see as rough play will give your dog the impression that they were in trouble, when they really weren't. Then, in future interactions, your dog might shy away from other big dogs and avoid being chased around.

On the other hand, don't shove your dog into a big group of other dogs if your pup isn't interested. Dogs take in a lot of information by ob-

Photo Courtesy of
Norma Ryan

Photo Courtesy of
Laura Chaffin
Cimarron Frontier Doodles

serving non-verbal cues and smells. Your dog should have ample time to sniff out his peers before jumping in the game of chase. You also don't want other dogs to see your dog as a threat or an easy target. Let your dog introduce himself in his own time. Otherwise, he may be afraid of future encounters.

Sometimes, it can be hard to distinguish between fighting and normal dog play. This will be covered more in depth in the next chapter, but it's important to watch your dog's non-verbal cues to see how they're feeling. A wagging tail is a good sign that your dog is having fun. A tail between the legs shows that your dog is worried. Bared teeth and growling is a sign that a dog is not having fun and is very upset.

Having your dog get along well with other dogs will make your life so much easier. When you go outside to get some exercise, you won't have to worry about your dog cowering in fear when another dog passes, or snapping at another dog at the park. Your dog will have an easier time focusing in training classes and will have an overall better quality of life if he can interact with his own kind.

Photo Courtesy of
Maureen Simpson
Arizona Goldendoodles

Properly Greeting New People

Part of being well-socialized is the ability to greet humans without getting nervous or upset. Generally speaking, Goldendoodles are very friendly and good with people. However, it only takes one bad encounter to scare your dog and make him nervous for future interactions. Dogs respond strongly to the feedback they receive from an action. Like with training, if a dog can associate something good with an action, they will repeat the action. If they receive a negative result, they will display avoidance behaviors. For example, if a dog lived in a previous home with an owner that yelled and hit him, he might not trust new people because he learned that interacting with people causes pain and fear.

HELPFUL TIP
Therapy Dogs

While service dogs undergo extensive training to be able to assist disabled persons with specific tasks, therapy dogs have a different mission. Therapy dogs accompany their owners to volunteer at schools, hospitals, nursing homes, libraries, and other locations where many people can benefit from the dog's presence. From bringing joy to lonely people to helping children learn to read, therapy dogs can be a valuable part of any community. Due to their social nature, intelligence, and gentle temperament, Goldendoodles can be excellent therapy dogs. While there are several organizations which certify therapy dogs, therapy dogs are not service dogs and do not have the same privileges when flying on airplanes or entering restaurants, for example.

Similarly, your dog may be wary of someone who looks unfamiliar. If you are a small woman and your dog is used to people who look like you, your dog may be nervous around a very large man. Some dogs are cautious around people who look different than the people they're used to. Introducing your dog to a wide variety of people will help them understand that people can be trusted.

When introducing your dog to strangers, do so slowly. You may want to invite everyone you know to your house after you bring your dog home to show off his cuteness, but this may be too overwhelming for a dog. Introduce him to a few people at a time. Have your guests sit down and let your dog come to them. Allow your dog to sniff them out before trying to pet him. Then, have your guests offer treats to your dog. This will reinforce the idea that being friendly around humans is good.

If you have an especially cautious dog, take this introduction thing to the next level. While out on a walk, or at a dog park, find willing strangers to offer treats to your dog. You'll find that people will be more than

willing to help out because they get to pet your adorable Goldendoodle. Give a treat to a stranger and ask them to approach your dog. If your dog is polite, tell them to give the treat to your dog. Your Goldendoodle may be able to tell the difference between your friends and a friendly stranger, so by involving people you don't know, your dog will feel more at ease when passing an unknown person.

Goldendoodles and Kids

If you have a family, a Goldendoodle is a great addition! This breed loves to run around and have fun with kids. However, kids behave very differently than adults, so it's good to give your dog some exposure to children in a controlled setting. This type of socialization is the same as socialization with adult humans, but with more monitoring and educating.

If kids haven't had a lot of experience with dogs, they may not know how to behave. Similarly, a dog might not know how to behave around kids. Kids can be overly energetic at times, which may get a dog riled up, too. Sometimes, this excess energy may cause dogs to play a little too roughly with kids. If this happens and the children are concerned, have them stop what they're doing and give the dog some time to settle down. Or, if the kids play too roughly and the dog is getting worried, teach your kids to recognize the signs of an anxious dog and instruct them to give the dog some space. Teach them how to nicely pet a dog and stay away from sensitive areas.

As the owner, it's your responsibility to make sure everyone is safe when interacting with your dog, including your dog. Even if you feel as though your dog can be trusted around your kids, and vice versa, it's still important to be around in case something goes wrong. Dogs have limited means of communication with their people, so if they become extremely uncomfortable, they may snap without little warning. Or, they'll give warning, but kids don't have the experience to interpret it. In general, you shouldn't have to worry about a well-socialized, well-bred Goldendoodle having a problem with anyone, but it's better to be safe than sorry. Once your dog learns how to act around kids, and your kids learn how to act around the dog, they will be the best of friends!

Socialization takes a lot of exposure to different people and dogs in different settings. It's important to get out into the world and teach your dog how to behave around others early in their life. Make sure that you can give your dog as many positive experiences as possible. Treats and encouragement are a must when it comes to teaching your dog to trust others. This type of training can be a lot of fun for both you and your dog, and requires little work for you—all you have to do is get out into the world and have fun with your dog, and they'll be a better dog because of it!

CHAPTER 8
Goldendoodles and Your Other Pets

If you're planning on adding another dog to your pack, a Goldendoodle is a good choice. This breed is friendly and gets along well with other dogs, especially compared to some breeds that are better suited as only dogs. While your Goldendoodle may have no problem joining the party, your other pets may have some reservations. With a little preparation, your pets will accept your new Goldendoodle with no issues.

Introducing Your New Puppy to Your Other Pets

"When you first bring a puppy home to a house with other pets, leave the puppy in a crate. Allow the other pets to become acquainted with him. This keeps the puppy feeling safe from any aggression and possible scarring. If the other pets are showing positive vibes, after a while tether them and allow the puppy to approach at his discretion and with your supervision."

Laura Chaffin
Cimarron Frontier Doodles

Photo Courtesy of Jennifer Yu

As mentioned in an earlier chapter, it should take some time for your pets to become acquainted. Best-case scenario, your pets will get along well from the very start. The more likely situation is that your pets take a little time to warm up to each other, then become pals. In order to prevent any issues between pets, there are a few ways to ease into this new friendship.

HELPFUL TIP
Goldendoodle Guard Dog?

Though Goldendoodles tend to be large dogs, they are not known for being particularly good guard dogs. This is generally because of their reputation for being friendly, affable dogs with a mild temperament. Though they may not be good guard dogs, Goldendoodles' intelligence can make them excellent watch dogs to alert their owners of visitors.

First, try to make your first meeting on neutral ground. Dogs can be territorial creatures and can feel protective over their domain. When another dog comes into their territory, they may respond poorly to the invader. To take care of this issue, try to meet up at a friend's house or at a park. Once your dogs get along in a neutral space, you can try another introduction in your home.

It's helpful to have some assistance with this process. Have a friend hold the leash for one dog while you hold the other. This way, if trouble arises, you can quickly separate the dogs. You might even try taking the dogs on a walk together so they can be in close proximity, but not necessarily directly interacting.

Once your pets begin to get acquainted with one another, you can increase the amount of time they spend together. However, remember to let them interact naturally and don't force them to be in a close space if they're more comfortable doing their own thing in opposite sides of the yard. When they're ready to play, they will. When you bring your new Goldendoodle home for good, make sure there are always opportunities for your pets to separate themselves, if necessary. For example, don't leave your cat and your Goldendoodle in a closed room without supervision, even if they've gotten along in the past. You never know what will set an animal off when you're not looking, and they need to be able to make space between each other for their own safety. For a cat, a cat tree works well. For dogs, a spacious room or baby gates can give your dogs a little more space to feel secure.

Pack Mentality

Photo Courtesy of Denise Tkacik

There is some controversy as to whether today's domesticated dogs behave like their canine ancestors. Some trainers believe that dogs continue to carry out specific roles within a pack, while others believe that our dogs are too far removed from their wild relatives for this to be a reliable method for understanding dogs. Whether dogs are pack-minded or not is up for debate, but we may still be able to understand why our dogs behave the way they do by examining how the dog pack operates.

Every dog pack has a leader. The other dogs in the pack look to the leader for direction and fall in line. Some dogs are more dominant than others, while some are quite passive. This social hierarchy doesn't really affect how aggressive or meek a dog is, nor does it make one dog in the pack happier than the other. When dogs live and travel together, they need someone to make decisions for the rest of the pack.

In your dog pack, the owner should be seen as the leader. If your dog constantly looks to you for direction, then you know you've accomplished this. To lead your dog pack, you don't need to be harsh or aggressive. Be firm when your dog is acting up, but be kind and loving. Going on walks can be a great time to teach your dog how to follow you and look to you for direction. Later chapters will discuss walking etiquette.

Because dogs fall in different spots along the hierarchy, you'll notice that the dogs in your home sometimes act according to this social order. You may have one dog that doesn't like when the other dog eats food first. In the dog pack, the alpha is the first one to eat. Or, you'll notice that one dog is more reserved and yields to the other. This is perfectly acceptable behavior. The only thing that is not acceptable is fighting. However, aggression has nothing to do with a dog pack mentality, and has more to do with fear.

According to Amie Paulson of Clovie's Creation kennel, it's okay to let your established dog put your new dog in their place when the puppy crosses a line. Your old dog might seem annoyed when your puppy is going wild and trying to climb all over them. An adult dog may give your puppy a little nip to tell the puppy that their behavior is not acceptable in their pack. As long as your established dog doesn't hurt your puppy, your puppy will learn proper behavior from their elders.

Fighting and Aggressive Behavior

It can be very scary if your dog gets into a fight, either with your own dog or a dog at the park. It's also dangerous to intervene in a fight because dogs can do a lot of damage with their strong jaws and sharp teeth. Your dog would never deliberately hurt you, but in the heat of the moment, they might not know it's you tugging on them, and bite you because they think you're another dog in the fight. Still, you will need to stop the fightand keep everyone in your household safe.

Never get in the face of a fighting dog. If your hands reach too close to teeth, you're bound to get a bite. Instead, give yourself some room on the leash and give your dog a firm and quick pull backward. Instead of tugging like a game of tug-of-war, give it a sharp pop to get your dog's attention. If your dog is not on a leash, try grabbing their back legs and walk backward. Not only does this keep you away from teeth, but it makes it hard for your dog to fight. Some owners will also place barriers between their dogs so they break their intense stare, like a baking sheet. Others will rattle a can full of rocks to get the dogs' attention away from

each other. Whatever you do, try to break their concentration, get the dogs apart, and keep yourself out of harm's way.

Once the fight is over, keep the dogs away from each other for a little while to give them time and space to cool down. When you bring the dogs back together, keep an eye on them and watch out for any aggressive behavior. If you spot any aggression warning signs, like growling or staring, separate the dogs again. If this issue doesn't resolve itself, you may need to discuss your options with a trainer or behavioral specialist.

Littermates

If one Goldendoodle is good, are two Goldendoodles better? If the puppies come from the same litter, you might not have double the fun. When littermates are purchased together, they tend to display strange behaviors that you wouldn't find in dogs from different litters. Littermates can be extremely clingy and get upset if they are separated. This can cause problems if you have to take one dog to the vet, and not the other. They also will distract each other and have a hard time paying attention when it comes to training. Some trainers won't even allow littermates in their classes because they can be so disruptive.

If you want to have multiple Goldendoodles in your home, you might want to wait a little bit between dogs. That way, you won't experience dogs with "littermate syndrome," nor will you have to go through the struggle of housetraining and obedience training two puppies at the same time.

What to Do If My Pets Don't Get Along

If you try and try to get your dogs to get along, but they just won't, you'll have to come up with a plan. Even if you do everything right when it comes to socialization, some animals just don't mix very well. Perhaps you have an old cat in your home that swats at your Goldendoodle at every opportunity. Or, maybe your old dog is just one of those breeds that doesn't get along with other dogs. If your pets don't get along to the point where one or more is at danger of getting hurt or suffering excessive stress, it's important to do something before things get out of hand.

The first thing you might want to try is to work with a trainer or other type of animal specialist. These experts might have some ideas for you to try to help your pets get along. Some trainers will even come to your house to diagnose the problem and help you work with your pets. Once they understand your situation, they may be able to tell you if it's possible to keep all of the pets in your home.

If this doesn't work, you may have to make a tough decision. You don't want anyone to get hurt. Perhaps it's not the best time for a new puppy. Maybe when your household circumstances are different, you'll be able to bring in a new puppy. Until then, it may be best to keep your house as is. It can be hard to come to this conclusion, but just remember that you're doing the right thing for all animals involved.

Goldendoodles make a great addition to your home because they get along well with everyone. In order to make everyone feel comfortable, give your pets plenty of time to adjust and get to know one another. In time, your little dog pack should be getting along just fine. If not, do your best to defuse the tension between your pets. A dog trainer can give you tips and even come into your home and see what the problem is. It's rare to have problems with Goldendoodles, but always remember to keep your pets' best interests in mind.

Photo Courtesy of
Bev Eckert
Hilltop Pups

CHAPTER 9
Exercise

"Most people group Goldendoodles with Labradoodles and assume that they have the same high energy as a Labradoodle. While they do have some energy and like to play, they do not have near the energy or require as much activity as a Labradoodle."

Kristine Probst
Island Grove Pet Kennels

Goldendoodles are energetic dogs that love to run around and play. So, this breed isn't great for people who don't spend a lot of time at home, or aren't willing or able to walk or run with their pup. However, an energetic dog is the perfect motivation for getting more exercise for you, too. Still, this breed's big puppy eyes can't always convince you to get off of the couch or come home from work on time. The Goldendoodle owner should have some motivation to get moving with their dog.

According to Amie Paulson of Clovie's Creation, a tired dog is a good dog. This means that dogs are better behaved and less destructive when they've had some sort of energy output throughout the day, as opposed to a dog that's been cooped up in the house for hours. You'll find that your Goldendoodle is much more obedient and less anxious when he's had some time to play.

STORY
Surf's Up!

Some owners are finding clever ways to include canine companions in their athletic endeavors. A man in Prior Lake, Minnesota, recently taught his one-and-a-half-year-old miniature Goldendoodle, Bella, how to kneeboard! Bella's owner, Mike Thibault, is an avid water-skier and wanted to include his dog in the fun.

Just like with people, exercise keeps your Goldendoodle happy and healthy. Without a way to burn calories, your dog may pack on the pounds, contributing to disease. Also, a dog's good mental health requires different types of stimulation. A dog that never gets to leave the house will become bored and will become destructive to entertain himself.

Photo Courtesy of
Caitlin Sharpe

Exercise Requirements

The amount of exercise a dog needs varies from breed to breed. Because Goldendoodles are medium to large dogs with lots of energy, they need more exercise than most dogs. Over time, you'll start to figure out how much exercise your dog needs to be well-behaved. Until you get to know your Goldendoodle's needs, start with an hour or so in the morning, and the same in the evening.

An hour of exercise, two times a day, doesn't mean that you'll have to be running alongside your dog for that entire period. There are a lot of different things you can do with your dog that don't require strenuous exercise on your part. It's also good for your dog to vary the type of

Photo Courtesy of Traci Wolos

exercise he gets. This keeps your dog entertained and on his toes.

For example, you may be short on time in the morning as you get ready for your day. So, you can start by taking your dog on a twenty-minute walk or jog. As you drink your morning coffee, play a game of fetch with your Goldendoodle. You can stay in one place as your dog sprints across the yard, chasing the ball.

This period of exercise doesn't need to be contained within the hour, either. If you only have thirty minutes to devote to your dog in the morning, you can always come home at lunchtime and play another quick game of fetch. If that doesn't work with your schedule, you can hire a dog walker to make sure your pup gets some fresh air midday. Or, maybe your dog likes to chase squirrels in your fenced-in yard. Ten minutes of running around chasing wildlife counts as exercise, and requires no work from you. Goldendoodle experts recommend a couple of hours of exercise a day, but you can be creative with how your dog gets this exercise.

Different Types of Exercise to Try

Goldendoodles are great because they are generally down for everything. This breed loves to walk, run, play, and even swim. So, there is no shortage of things you can do with your dog! To keep your dog entertained, try to switch up the exercise your dog gets. If walking the same routes gets boring for both of you, try going to a big dog park and launching a tennis ball as far as you can throw. Or, teach your dog a new game, like Frisbee. This breed can learn new skills very easily, so there's no limit to what your dog can do.

Walking and running are old standards. While you may get bored when you walk the same route a few days in a row, your dog will stay entertained with all of the new smells. Walks also allow dogs to spend time around other people, animals, and new settings, which helps your dog acclimate to new places. Even though it may seem as though your Goldendoodle can walk or run forever, make sure to carry water with you on long adventures and pay special attention to signs that they are getting tired. Dogs are sprinters, not long-distance runners. While humans can handle distances over five miles, a dog doesn't need to run more than three or four. When it's hot out, go shorter distances or risk having to carry your pooch back home. Dogs don't sweat like humans do, so they can get overheated when undergoing too much exertion in hot temperatures.

Photo Courtesy of
Tammara Ruesink

*Photo Courtesy of
Logan Schuering*

When it's too hot to walk, try taking your dog swimming. Paddling around the shallow water in a lake can burn a lot of energy, and Goldendoodles love splashing along the beach. You can even incorporate a game of fetch into the activity by throwing a floating toy into the water. Be careful when sending your dog out into the water, no matter how strong a swimmer they are. Some dogs will swim away from shore, only to get tired and have trouble returning. Also, streams and oceans may carry your dog further away from you than you'd like. A shallow, still body of water may be safer for your pup. There are also life jackets made just for dogs that will keep your pup afloat. Even if your dog is a proficient paddler, it's always good to strap one on your dog to keep them safe.

Playing games in the backyard is a fun, interactive way to spend time with your dog. Goldendoodles are excellent at fetch and will play for hours if you let them. These games also teach valuable skills, like "drop it" and "take it." If you don't have a powerful arm to throw the ball, there are fun products in pet stores that can help you fling the ball further so your dog can burn more zooms. Frisbee is a similar game that requires some skill from both owner and dog. Buy a Frisbee from a pet store that's softer than the hard plastic humans play catch with. Then, work on throwing it so your dog can easily catch it in his mouth. When he's successful, give him lots of praise. This will reinforce the idea that catching the Frisbee is good, motivating him to run faster and leap higher to catch it.

Fun Indoor Games for Energetic Dogs

Sometimes the weather doesn't allow for you and your dog to get outdoor exercise. Instead of letting your dog go stir-crazy inside your home, there are a few things you can do to keep your dog active and entertained. Goldendoodles are intelligent dogs, so they also need mental stimulation, as well as physical exertion. While it's easier to throw a ball around the yard than to come up with ideas for indoor exercise, especially if you have a smaller home, there are still plenty of things you can do with your Goldendoodle when you can't go outside.

One game that keeps your dog active for a long time is hide and seek. This takes some prior knowledge of commands, but once your dog learns the rules, you'll have lots of fun playing. Start with your dog in the sit and stay position on one side of the house. Then, take a favorite toy and hide it in another room, so your dog can't see where you're hiding it. Return to your dog and tell him to find the object, and watch as he goes to work, sniffing around for his favorite toy. When he eventually retrieves it, give lots of praise and treats, and repeat the process for as long as your dog is willing to play. This game keeps your dog moving, as well as their mind.

*Photo Courtesy of
Abby Hosman*

Tug is another game that can be played in a small space that can burn energy. Hold on tightly to one end of a rope toy and let your dog take the other end. Pull on your end and gently move the rope side to side to tap into your dog's playful instincts. They will pull against you with all of their might until they win the game. As an added bonus, the rope toy will help clean your dog's teeth as he chews. This game is best played in a carpeted area, as a tile floor doesn't have the traction your dog needs for a good, solid tug. If you find your dog gets too wound up by this game, stop whenever you've had enough. Your dog will learn to play games by your rules, not his.

Any kind of dog training is also a good way to keep your dog entertained when you can't go outside. With the right treats, your dog will sit, stay, and crawl all over your house. Rainy and snowy days are a great time to stay in and work on obedience skills and learn new tricks. Then, when the weather is better, you can spend all of your free time playing Frisbee and fetch.

It's also a good idea to look into indoor dog parks and dog clubs with indoor facilities. If your dog has some agility training, you may be able to practice crawling through tunnels and jumping over obstacles on your own time. Other dog sports, like nose work and flyball, are good activities for Goldendoodles to take part in, as they can be practiced indoors. An energetic breed like the Goldendoodle will want to stretch their legs, so any indoor opportunity they can get to run and play is helpful for the owner's sanity. Of course, if it's possible to go outside for a short period of time, do. Even ten to twenty minutes of walking around the neighborhood will improve your dog's overall disposition and behavior.

While it's easy to skip a dog walking or leave your dog in the yard alone to wander around, allowing your dog to stay idle is not good for your dog or your relationship with your dog. A bored and energetic dog creates problems for your household. A tired dog is a good dog, and you'll find this to be the case when you just want to get some work done around the house, or you want to take your dog to a training class.

There are so many fun things that you can do with your Goldendoodle that neither of you should become tired of your daily exercise. Check out new places on your daily walks and enjoy the time you spend with your dog as you throw a Frisbee for your Goldendoodle to catch. Take your Goldendoodle on fun outings to swim in a lake or go hiking. When the weather doesn't allow you to go outside, come up with new activities to get your Goldendoodle off the couch and using his brain. Exercise is an important part of your dog's day, and plenty of fun activities will make your Goldendoodle a happy and healthy pup.

CHAPTER 10
Training Your Goldendoodle

"Goldendoodles are GIGO dogs. Instead of 'Garbage In, Garbage Out', they are Good In, Good Out - the limitations to what they can accomplish are determined by the time and training they receive."

Jennifer Tramell
Music City Goldendoodles

Goldendoodles are intelligent dogs, which makes them easier to train than some other breeds. However, this does not mean that your Goldendoodle will magically understand your commands without a lot of training. The training process takes a lot of time and energy, but it is absolutely worth it when your dog follows your commands. Practice often, have patience, and before you know it, you'll have an obedient dog.

Clear Expectations

When it comes to teaching your dog appropriate behaviors for your home, it's good to have a clear set of expectations for your dog. You'll also want your family in on the rules you set forth for your Goldendoodle so your pup can have some consistency in his training. For example, you'll want to use the same cue words for the same command every time. If you want your dog to stop jumping up on you, but you use "down" and "off" interchangeably, your dog won't know if he's supposed to put four paws on the floor or get on his belly.

Or, your idea of a perfectly completed command might be different from your family members'. When you put your dog into the sit position, it is implied that your dog will hold that position until you give further direction. Therefore, if your dog gets up a second after sitting, the command has been broken. But, if another trainer in your home gives a reward if your dog's bottom hits the floor, your dog may receive mixed signals about what he's supposed to do when he hears "sit."

For this reason, it's great to have the whole family attend training classes. That way, everyone has the same understanding of the commands and how to give them. Goldendoodles are intelligent dogs, but they don't have the ability to reason like humans do. If they're exposed to inconsistency in their training, prepare to have inconsistent results.

*Photo Courtesy of
Maureen Simpson
Arizona Goldendoodles*

Operant Conditioning Basics

Dog training is based around the psychological concept of operant conditioning. However, this doesn't mean that you have to be a psych major to learn how to train a dog. When working with your Goldendoodle, it's important to think like a dog. It's easy to project our human learning processes on your furry friend, but it won't help you understand why your dog does the things he does.

In short, operant conditioning uses a system of rewards to shape your dog's behavior. When you teach your dog a trick, they don't use logic or reason to understand it. Instead, they are merely conditioned to do the motion because they have learned that good things happen when they do what their owner commands them to do.

The reinforcements for the dog's behavior can be positive or negative, though dogs respond better to positive reinforcement than negative reinforcement. When your dog does something you like, you give them some sort of reward for their behavior. Over time, this signals to your dog that their action is good, and that they should continue to do it. Eventually, you will no longer even need to give rewards for each successful command because your dog will be "programmed" to complete the task.

While each command requires different methods to teach it, all dog training follows the concept of operant conditioning. If you can put your dog into a desired position and give them a reward for doing so, you can teach your Goldendoodle almost anything. Repetition is key here, because your dog needs enough exposure to the command for it to stick in his brain.

Primary Reinforcements

Primary reinforcements are simply rewards that hold immediate value. Food, toys, and play are examples of primary reinforcements used in dog training. These rewards are given to your dog when they do something desirable. This lets them know that they did something right, and should continue to do so when prompted.

Food is perhaps the most enticing of all the primary reinforcements when it comes to dog training. Dogs can't resist the smell of a special treat, and they will do just about anything to get it. The most effective dog treats are ones that are strongly scented and are small enough to give plenty of in one training session. Small, moist treats are easier to train with than big milkbones that take a while to eat. Some owners will even use small slices of hot dogs because it's a special treat for a dog. All dogs have their own preferences when it comes to food. Some will gobble down just anything, while others are pickier. When selecting a training treat, find something that makes your dog lick his chops when you open the bag.

While most dogs are food-driven, some respond more to toys. If your dog is not strongly motivated by food, that doesn't mean they can't be trained. Instead, you have to come up with creative rewards for good behavior. If your dog ignores treats, but goes wild for a good squeaky toy, use that enthusiasm to your advantage. Sometimes this playful breed just wants to have a good time, and this natural playfulness should be used to your advantage.

For example, your dog may not come to you when you have a treat in your hand, but they'll positively ambush you when you show them their favorite toy. In this situation, teach the command per usual, but hand over the toy when they successfully complete it. Then, they can have some quick playtime before they return the toy to you and you go back to training mode.

At the end of your training session, you want to give your dog some playtime to let them know that they've done a good job. Training shouldn't last terribly long, and a little play helps release them from the work mindset. Dogs can get bored if you drill them with the same commands for too long, so some play will keep training fun and positive.

Secondary Reinforcements

Primary reinforcements are rewards that are good in and of themselves. Secondary reinforcements are rewarding because there is some value attached to them. For dogs, praise and clickers are useful secondary reinforcements. These rewards don't offer immediate payout like a tasty treat does, but they can be connected with primary reinforcements. Think of secondary reinforcements like currency for dogs—dogs have no use for the currency itself, but it yields the primary reinforcements that they love.

Praise is a reward that should be used constantly when training your dog. Goldendoodles are sensitive creatures and aim to please, so your love and affection lets them know that they're doing a good job. Also, an affirmative voice marker, like "good" or "yes," can even be used instead of a treat. To do this, you must start out by giving your dog a treat for good behavior, along with the affirmative marker. Over time, your dog will be conditioned to hear your affirmations and understand them as rewarding. Whenever your dog does something right, make them feel like they're the best dog in the whole world. This will help them attach positive feelings to their training, and make them more likely to absorb new commands.

Clicker training is a similar concept that's popular with dog owners. A clicker is a small, handheld device that emits a clicking sound when you press the button. When the sound is associated with treats or other primary rewards, your dog will hear the sound and accept it as a reward. The clicker also adds precision to your training. When you hand over a treat for a successful command, the time it takes between reaching toward your dog and your dog's acceptance of the treat makes it hard to reward very specific actions. With the clicker, you can give them a reward in a split second. For example, if your dog is just learning how to sit and stay, you can reward your dog with the clicker when they manage to stay for a few seconds. When you try to hand over a treat, your dog may break their sit to reach for their snack.

If you don't have a clicker, a voice marker (like "yes") can work in its place. But a clicker can be an inexpensive training tool that will help reward your dog for good behavior. When using secondary reinforcements, remember to pair them with a primary reinforcement for maximum effectiveness. Otherwise, your dog will have a lot of "cash" that he doesn't have any use for. When training, give rewards often, and make sure they are of high value to your pup.

Dangers of Negative Reinforcement

Negative reinforcement, or punishment, is part of operant conditioning, but it doesn't mean that it should be used while training your dog. Goldendoodles are especially sensitive dogs, so anything upsetting may set your dog back in their training. Also, dogs respond to negativity with avoidance and you can't always predict how they're going to avoid negativity.

For instance, if your dog is being naughty, you may scold them and command them to your side. Then, you'll probably take away whatever fun activity they were doing when you got angry. You may think that the scolding will deter them from the bad behavior, but instead, your dog may associate the come command with negativity. Then, when you're working on recall, your dog will not want to come to you because he thinks he'll be scolded. For this reason, it's important to think like a dog, and predict their behavioral outcomes if you apply any sort of negative reinforcement.

In more severe cases, owners may swat or scream at their dog for unwanted behaviors. After a while, the dog will become afraid of the owner. In most cases, a fearful dog will not want to spend time around the owner, much less work on training, where there could be more punishments. Worst-case scenario, a dog could be so fearful that he snaps back and injures someone. There is often a fine line between punishment and abusive behavior that can result in worse behaviors from your dog. It's best to keep training as positive as possible, and avoid all punishment whenever possible. The next chapter will discuss how to deal with unwanted behaviors in a manner that will not harm your dog.

Hiring a Trainer

Dog trainers are an invaluable resource, especially if you're working with your first dog. A trainer will teach you how to train your dog and give you the skills you need to continue working with your Goldendoodle after the classes have concluded. Regular classes also provide owners with motivation to practice frequently with their dogs so they can come to the next lesson with mastered skills. Meanwhile, your Goldendoodle gets the opportunity to interact with new people and dogs. There are more benefits to hiring a professional trainer than just dog training.

There are different types of classes and trainers to choose from. Perhaps the most common type of professional training comes from a group course. These classes are broken down into different skill levels and training needs. These classes are generally small groups of dogs (and their humans) and meet regularly until the course is complete. Once you complete one class, you can choose to move onto the next one, which helps to keep up your rigorous training schedule.

Another option is to hire a personal dog trainer. This is useful if you have a schedule that makes it hard to attend regular classes, or you have a specific issue you want to work on. These trainers are more expensive than the fee you might pay for a group class, but it's worth it if you have specific training needs you can't meet in a traditional training class. Some dog trainers will even travel to your home to help diagnose issues in your Goldendoodle's behavior, or work on your schedule for convenience. However, you'll miss out on valuable socialization time, especially if your Goldendoodle is still a young pup.

Owner Behavior

One overlooked aspect of dog training is the owner's behavior. Goldendoodles look to their owners for how to think and feel. So, if you're calm and positive, they'll be calm. If you're frustrated or anxious, they'll think they need to worry, too.

Dog training can be tough at times. There will be moments when your Goldendoodle just doesn't want to cooperate. Or, there will be other distracting factors that will make it hard for your dog to concentrate on his training. Your dog will take no time at all to learn some commands, while others will

STORY
Famous Goldendoodle

In the recent Hollywood Blockbuster, A Star is Born, a furry star shares the stage with Lady Gaga and Bradley Cooper. This dog, Charlie, has a charming backstory as Bradley Cooper's real-life rescue dog and is reported to be a Goldendoodle. Named after Cooper's father, Charlie has warmed the hearts of thousands of moviegoers. Goldendoodles are extremely intelligent and loyal dogs, so, given Cooper's established relationship with Charlie, it makes sense that he would cast his canine companion in this movie.

take months of practice. Because dogs can be so unpredictable and difficult to get through to, you're bound to feel frustrated at some point. However, it's important to keep your emotions in check. If you find yourself getting frustrated while training, take a break and come back to it when you've relaxed. Your Goldendoodle needs a happy and positive environment to fully enjoy training. A dog that loves to learn new tricks is a pleasure to work with, as opposed to a dog that dreads training time and avoids it at all costs.

Once you've mastered the basics of dog training theory, you can apply these concepts to any command or behavior. It takes a little time to get to know your Goldendoodle, but before long, you'll be able to think like a dog. When training your Goldendoodle, give your dog plenty of rewards so they'll become conditioned to complete the commands. Food and toys are great rewards, but don't forget to pair them with auditory markers that can be used when you're all out of treats. Finally, don't forget to use your resources. There are a lot of great dog trainers out there with a wealth of knowledge. The right resources and the right attitude will make dog training easy and fun.

CHAPTER 11
Dealing with Unwanted Behaviors

"I have found that a Goldendoodle's prey drive is one trait that is usually unwanted. This can show up as being difficult with feline members of the family as well as other small family pets."

Laura Chaffin
Cimarron Frontier Doodles

Photo Courtesy of
Nikolaj Schmidt Jensen

At some point in your relationship with your Goldendoodle, he will do something that you do not like. It can be as simple as digging a hole in your garden, or as serious as showing aggression toward other pets. No matter what the problem is, bad behavior should be corrected immediately and often. Life is simply easier when your dog is a good citizen and a good family member. This chapter will cover the different bad behaviors you may witness and give you ideas for how to solve these problems.

What Is Bad Behavior in Dogs?

Bad behavior is often in the eye of the owner. Tolerable dog behaviors differ from household to household. With human children, parents must decide how they want their children to behave, and then consistently raise them to that particular standard. Raising a dog is similar in that regard, but the issues at hand are much different!

Some dog owners will not tolerate some behaviors, while others are more lenient with their Goldendoodles. For example, one owner might be very strict about their dog barking, while another will let it slide if their dog is out in the backyard. Or, one owner may ban their dog from jumping on the couch, while another prefers their dog to cuddle with them at night. With benign behaviors like these, you're in no way a bad

*Photo Courtesy of
Ira Selwin*

Photo Courtesy of Sara Hester

dog owner if you let some naughtiness slide. Part of dog ownership is choosing your battles, especially with an intelligent breed like the Goldendoodle that may want to make their own rules.

Unwanted behaviors can be categorized by their level of severity. Annoying behaviors are any kind of unwanted behavior that causes minor inconvenience. Barking, jumping up on people, and begging for table scraps are all examples of annoying behaviors. These are the behaviors where the owner can decide which will be allowed and which will not.

Destructive behaviors are ones that ruin property. Digging and chewing are major culprits in this category. These are the types of dog activities that can cost the dog owner more in household damages than dog care itself. While all dogs will chew, destruction of property is extremely avoidable.

Finally, dangerous behaviors are ones that put your dog and others at risk of injury. These behaviors are serious and require immediate attention. Car chasing, running away, fighting, and any signs of aggression fall into this category. Behaviors that make your dog a risk to others must be handled immediately, or the consequences could be extreme. The last thing you want is for your dog to hurt someone, and for you to be responsible.

In the early days of having your Goldendoodle at home, think about what behaviors you want to avoid, and give yourself some extra time to observe your dog's habits and quirks. This way, you can make a plan of how to deal with these issues so you don't feel frantic when your dog is suddenly ripping apart your couch cushions.

Finding the Root of the Problem

Dog training requires you to think like a dog. You may have no idea why your dog stares out the window and barks at absolutely nothing, but that's because you can't hear the mail truck that's four blocks away. You may be baffled as to how your pup could possibly chew through the legs of your dining room chairs, but you forget that they get bored when you're gone all day and they're teething. Some dog behaviors will make no sense to you until you stop to think about the cause of it. It takes some time to get to know your dog's train of thought, but you'll eventually learn to see the world through their eyes. Then, you can figure out what's winding them up, and find ways to keep them calm.

Photo Courtesy of Jewell
Jewels Puppy Paws

If your dog has issues when dealing with people or other dogs, perhaps the issue is the way they were socialized. These problems may be more common in adopted dogs because someone else was in charge of the socialization work. Plus, your adopted dog may have been surrendered because he didn't do well in a home with other dogs or young children. Also, you never know what kind of care your dog was given in their previous home. It's entirely possible that neglect or mistreatment caused fear or aversions.

Some bad behaviors are a result of canine instinct. If your dog is digging holes all over your yard, can you deduce a specific reason for that behavior? Some dogs dig because they're trying to hunt animals in the ground, while others dig a nest to stay cool in hot temperatures. Your dog is probably not trying to be deliberately naughty, but acting in a way that aligns with his survival instinct.

Goldendoodles are good about being in tune with their owner's emotions. This breed generally aims to please, so they're not being bad to spite you, or anything like that. Dogs need to learn how to behave in the human home, which has much different rules than the dog den. It takes some time to fix these bad behaviors, but once you understand the reasoning behind their actions, it's easier to correct them.

Bad Behavior Prevention

HELPFUL TIP
Puzzle Toys

Goldendoodles are remarkably intelligent. While this is a desirable trait for many dog owners, it also makes for dogs that can become bored easily. Since unwanted dog behavior is often caused by boredom, puzzle toys may be an option for keeping your Goldendoodle entertained and out of trouble. Puzzle toys require your dog to solve a puzzle in order to retrieve a treat hidden inside the toy. These kinds of toys stimulate your dog's intelligence and help him get his all-important intellectual exercise.

When it comes to dealing with bad behavior, it's easier to prevent it than it is to correct it. Sometimes, owners unwittingly teach their dog bad behaviors, then have a hard time correcting them. You want to treat your Goldendoodle like a member of the family, but it's important to think about the potential consequences of certain actions.

For example, you may want to give your dog table scraps. Your puppy might look at you with their big eyes as you eat, and you'll give your dog a nibble of your leftovers. After all, it cuts down on food waste and it makes your best friend very happy. But then, your dog starts hanging out under the table while you eat, whining and begging for food. He might even jump up on the counter as you cook and steal ingredients because he knows that he's allowed to eat people food. Eventually, this begging will become a problem, especially when you have guests over and they can't eat in peace because your Goldendoodle is constantly whining and pawing underneath the table. All of this bad behavior could have been avoided by deciding to prohibit the feeding of table scraps.

Some behaviors can be predicted to the point that you can teach your dog certain behaviors to counteract bad ones. It's common for dogs to bark or rush the door when the doorbell rings. It's only natural that your friendly pup wants to greet the person or let you know that someone's at the door. Unfortunately, this behavior can be annoying to you and the people visiting your house. It can also wind your dog up into a frenzy because of how exciting it is when someone comes to the door. Even worse, some owners talk to their dog in a shrill, excited voice when someone's there, making the simple act of opening the door a big deal.

Instead of teaching your dog to get worked up when someone comes to the door, an owner can teach their dog to lie on their bed, or simply sit down at the sound of the doorbell. This can be done before any visitor ever arrives. That way, when someone comes over, you won't have to worry about your dog ambushing them.

You can't always predict how your Goldendoodle is going to act, but with some thinking ahead, you might be able to control how your actions affect your pooch. Goldendoodles look to their humans for direction, so many of the things you do will have a direct impact on their behavior.

How to Properly Correct Your Dog

While it's easy to explain to a child that running into traffic is dangerous and that you scold them because you don't want them to get hurt, it's hard to express these sentiments to a dog that can't speak your language. Dogs learn through conditioning, not reasoning, so you have to use the right tactics to correct bad behavior.

Photo Courtesy of Bev Eckert Hilltop Pups

When dealing with bad behavior, it's natural to feel annoyed or upset with your dog, especially if they've done something especially naughty. However, it's never acceptable to hit or scream at your dog. Instead of teaching your dog to behave properly, fear and pain will only cause your dog to avoid you, and could lead to more bad behaviors that are done out of distress. Patience and a controlled temper is important when dealing with bad behavior.

To correct bad behavior, you must first catch it. This requires a lot of attention from the owner. Correcting your dog after he has completed the behavior is not effective, so you must correct your dog by interrupting him. You can do this by getting his attention with a loud clap or a firm "hey!" When your dog breaks their focus on the bad behavior, gently redirect them to something more suitable, or give them praise and treats when they stop.

Chewing is a bad behavior that can be redirected. When you catch your puppy nibbling on the edge of the coffee table, clap loudly and get his attention. Once he stops and looks at you, give him a bone to chew on instead. If he accepts the bone, give him lots of praise. You'll have to repeat this process a few times, but your dog should eventually give up the wooden furniture and seek out the toys when he has the urge to chew.

Or, sometimes the correction is just a matter of stopping the bad behavior and replacing it with a new command. If your dog barks a lot, you may want to call attention to it by clapping your hands and diverting your dog's attention to you. If they're startled, they'll probably stop barking to figure out what's going on. When they're quiet, say "good no bark" and give them a treat. This way, you're teaching them that you like it when they're quiet, as opposed to barking. It can be difficult to correct bad habits, but if you stick with the training, your dog will learn to replace their bad behaviors with more acceptable ones.

When to Call a Professional

Training is challenging, but it can be even harder when you're teaching dogs not to do something. Mix that challenge with the fact that bad behaviors drive you up the wall, and it's no surprise that people get upset with their pets and ultimately give up on trying to change their behaviors. There's no shame in getting help if you're having a hard time with your dog. In fact, it makes you a better dog owner because you want your dog to be their very best!

If you've been taking classes with your Goldendoodle, a trainer is an excellent resource. They may not cover how to correct certain annoyances in obedience training, but your trainer will be more than happy to listen to your problems and offer advice. These trainers are experienced and have seen it all when it comes to dog behavior, so they'll likely have a few ideas for identifying problems or correcting behaviors.

If your dog is in danger of hurting a person or another dog, it is imperative that you do something about it. Because of the high risk involved, you may want to hire a personal dog trainer who specializes in these sorts of behaviors. This way, you aren't putting a class full of dogs at risk if yours becomes agitated. A veterinarian might also be able to see if your dog's behaviors are caused by a medical condition that can be treated. It's rare for Goldendoodles to show such aggressive traits, especially if they are well-bred and cared for, but dogs can be unpredictable at times and you'll want to ensure that no one is ever put in danger because of your dog.

Training your dog not to do things can be harder than teaching your dog new tricks. However, both use similar tactics. You must find a way to use conditioning to your advantage. Redirect your dog when they do something bad, and reward them when they do something well. Finally, know your limits. If you're so frustrated that you act out in anger, call in reinforcements. An experienced dog trainer may give you tips for dealing with the unwanted behaviors that drive you nuts. However, it's always important to remember that Goldendoodles are not purposefully trying to upset you; they are still learning how to live like a human in your home.

Photo Courtesy of LeeAnn Gott

CHAPTER 12
Basic Commands

While there are countless tricks you can teach your Goldendoo-dle, some are more important than others. Teaching your dog to roll over can be a lot of fun, but it's not a skill that's going to help you when you need to keep your dog safe or get them to settle down. There are a few basic commands that every dog should know so they can be a good canine citizen and family member. They are designed to keep your dog under control and safe, and other commands can be built upon this basic knowledge. Once you've mastered these basics, you can move on to the fun and challenging commands.

Benefits of Proper Training

Owning a Goldendoodle is a pleasure in itself, but life is so much easier when your dog actually does what you want them to do. You'll be amazed at how much better your relationship with your pup will be when you aren't constantly fighting them for control. It's not fun when you want to go on a nice walk, but your Goldendoodle is constantly pulling you in all different directions, nor is it enjoyable when your dog gets loose and runs as far away from you as possible. With the right training, you can keep your dog safe by your side.

An obedient dog is a dog that can go anywhere. A dog that knows how to listen to you can go to bars and restaurants and soak up the attention this breed gets. A well-behaved dog can be trusted to be good at the dog park and return to you when it's time to leave. A dog with the right training can sit still when you stop to tie your shoe, or can drop the dead bird they found in the backyard.

Intelligent dogs, like the Goldendoodle, need adequate mental stimulation or they'll become bored. Bored dogs tend to get themselves into trouble when trying to entertain themselves. Training is a great way to keep your dog's mind busy. You'll have a lot of fun watching your dog's mind work as they try to follow your verbal and non-verbal cues.

Places to Practice

One mistake that dog owners make when training their dog is only working with their pup in their home. These owners may master skills with their dog in their living room, but the dog fails to complete the command outside the home when it matters. Goldendoodles are sensitive to their surroundings; the distractions outside are much greater than the limited distractions in their usual territory. So, in order to train your dog to be well-rounded in their ability to successfully complete commands, you must change your practicing location on a regular basis.

Photo Courtesy of Jennifer Yu

The home is a good place to start because of the limited number of distractions. Your home has familiar sights, sounds, and smells, so your dog's mind won't be elsewhere while working. This is where you should introduce new commands and work on them while the information is still fresh.

Once your dog gets the hang of a command, take them to a new location. However, it's good to start slow. There's a big difference between your kitchen and a busy dog park. If you've been practicing indoors, your next step is to practice in your backyard, or out on the driveway. Once your dog shows proficiency, find a grassy area on one of your walking routes and practice their new skills. Once they prove they can listen to you, take them to the busy dog park or shopping mall. Keep challenging your dog until they can successfully complete commands in places with lots of distractions. In the end, your goal is to prepare your dog for any situation. If they will come to you when they're surrounded by exciting distractions, then they've mastered the command.

Basic Commands

Out of all the possible commands you can teach a dog, there are a handful that are more useful than the rest. These basic commands are designed to keep your dog at attention and out of trouble. Also, these commands provide a solid background on which you can build further knowledge. For example, a dog needs to learn how to lie down before he can learn how to roll over. But, once they learn how to lie down, they can then learn a whole new group of commands that start from the down position.

Also, even if you don't plan on training your Goldendoodle to become a trick aficionado, there are still skills they need to master to make life with a dog pleasant. The following tricks should be the bare minimum that you teach your dog. It's great to continue to challenge your dog, but if you only have the time and patience to teach a handful of commands, these are the ones you want to focus on.

Sit

This is perhaps the first command you'll teach your dog because it's easy for Goldendoodles to do and it's easy to teach. Even a little puppy can learn how to sit, although they may not hold the position for very long. This command can be used in so many different scenarios. When you need your dog to wait or calm down for a moment, sit is a good command to keep them quiet and still.

To teach this command, you'll want your dog in a standing position. Hold a treat in your hand and move it above and slightly past their nose. They should follow the treat with their nose, naturally causing them to sit. If this doesn't work, you can gently place your hand on their bottom and apply light pressure to show them what you want them to do. Once they hit the sitting position, give them a treat and lots of praise. After you've got the motion down, start adding the command "sit" before they sit. When they do this command, the implication is that they will remain seated until you give them further commands, or release them by saying, "okay."

STORY
First Goldendoodle Seeing Eye Dog

On April 23, 2003, at Fox Creek Farm in West Virginia, a Goldendoodle puppy named Richter was born. Richter would become the first Goldendoodle Seeing Eye dog. At eight weeks of age, Richter was donated to the Guide Dogs of America in California. He graduated from training on May 1st, 2005.

Down

Once you teach sit, you'll want to try "down." This will be more difficult than the sit command because your dog might feel uncomfortable being told to lie on the ground on command. But this is useful for times when you want your dog to chill out for a little longer than you might put them in a sit. It also takes them a little bit longer to spring into action from a down position, so when it's paired with a "stay" it will give them more time to chill out.

To teach this, start with your dog in the sit position. Hold the treat in front of their nose, then slowly move it toward the floor. They will follow the treat with the nose, but when it gets too close to the ground, they will naturally lower their body. You want your dog to go all the way to the floor. If they only go partway down, it's easy for them to spring back up. Once they are on the ground, give them their treat and praise.

If they have a hard time following the treat, you can try to gently nudge them into position with their leash. Try not to tug or force them down. Instead, gently apply downward pressure to the leash while moving the treat in front of their face to show them how to get into the down position. Once you have them where you want them, give them treats and praise.

Stay

This command can be challenging to teach, especially if you have an active puppy with a short attention span. However, it can come in handy if your Goldendoodle loves to roam around and get into trouble. The stay command is useful because when it's done right, your dog will freeze in place until they're given further instructions. If you find yourself in a situation where you need to leave your dog for a moment and don't want them to follow you, this command will come in handy.

To teach this, start with your dog in the "sit" position. This gives them the clue that they're supposed to be performing a certain action. Place your hand in front of their face like a stop sign and say, "stay." Walk back a few steps while holding out your palm, pause a moment, then return. If they're still motionless when you return, give them their reward. If they break, put them back into a sit and stay and try again.

When you're starting out, don't take more than a few steps away. Naturally, they're going to want to follow you. Over time, build up the distance between you and your pup. You can also add challenging variables like turning your back toward your dog, leaving the room, and even circling them. When you want to practice long distances in distracting environments, buy a twenty-foot leash to give your dog some extra distance while still keeping some control over them.

If your dog has a really tough time staying still, practice this command on a leash. That way, you can drop the leash and put a foot on it when they start to get up. This should "self-correct" and make it harder for them to move. Or, you might even want to start slower by putting them in a stay, and simply moving from their side to in front of them. Then, once they can stay still, face them and walk backward. At first, your Goldendoodle will want to follow you and stay by your side. Over time, they'll understand that you're going to return, and they'll relax a little.

Come

Being able to recall your dog is so important. Every once in a while, your dog is doing something they shouldn't be doing, and you need a way to get them close to your side. Or, you may encounter a dangerous situation and you need to protect your dog or keep them out of the way. If your Goldendoodle likes to wander, then the "come" command can save their life.

To teach this, put your dog in a sit and stay. When you're a few feet away, call your dog toward you. If you have a treat in your hand, your Goldendoodle will likely hear your enthusiastic voice, see your open arms, and come barreling toward you. When your dog comes to you, put a hand on their collar so they don't run away, and give them a treat.

If they don't run straight toward you, try nudging them along with their leash. When your dog is in the sit and stay, take the leash with you and call your dog. If they don't immediately come to you, give a gentle tug. This should redirect their attention to you, prompting them to approach you. They'll be more inclined to come to you if you are waiting for them with treats and praise.

Because you want your dog to come to you every time, avoid calling them if you're only going to yell at them. Our dogs do things to frustrate us, but the "come" command should not be used to recall your dog for punishment. If your dog learns that responding to "come" is not always a positive experience, they will not want to do it. If they have an unreliable recall, they may not respond to you when it really counts. For this reason, if your dog comes to you, make sure you give them tons of affection and praise so they will continue to do so.

Leash Training

Goldendoodles love to go on walks with their humans. It's a great way to get some exercise while spending quality time together. However, if your dog doesn't walk very well on a leash, walks will become a tedious chore that will leave you feeling frustrated. From the moment you clip the leash onto your dog's collar, it's time to start practicing good walking habits. The more you leash train with your dog in the early days, the happier you'll be in the long run. It's not natural for dogs to walk right next to you on a leash, especially if they're curious and love to explore. Quality practice is necessary for teaching your dog how to act polite on walks.

To start, your dog should be positioned on your left side. They should walk in line with you, not too far ahead and not lagging behind. There should not be any tension in the leash; it should hang loosely between you. When you stop, your dog should stop and sit by your side. When you turn, your dog should turn along with you, speeding up or slowing down to remain in position on your left side. Easier said than done, right?

It takes a ton of practice to get your dog to walk nicely. It's easy to give up on training and let your dog take control while he gets his exercise, but this behavior will get old very quickly. Good leash training will keep your dog in check and make walks much more pleasant.

Before you go on your walk, get your dog to sit on your left side. This will give you some consistency in your walks so your dog knows they have rules to follow. Plus, it will keep your dog from weaving back and forth. Hold the end of the leash with your right hand, and slide your left

*Photo Courtesy of
Jen Halbett*

hand down your leash to keep your dog close. Also, keep a lot of treats on hand because you'll need to give out rewards every time your dog walks nicely.

Say, "let's go" and take a few steps forward. If they walk alongside you without pulling, give them tons of praise and a treat. It helps to talk to your dog while you walk, so their focus is on you. Tell them about how good they're being. When you talk to your dog, they should look up at you. A dog that looks at you while you walk will look to you for direction. If they start to pull or get distracted, give a quick tug on the leash to remind them what they need to do. Don't yank too hard or drag your dog. Instead, a quick pop will help keep them in line without hurting them. When there is slack on the leash again, praise and reward them.

Once you've got the walking thing down, practice changing your pace. Slow down and direct your dog to do the same. Or, speed up and get your dog really moving. Work on right turns, left turns, and about-faces. Halt suddenly and have your dog sit beside you. Instruct your dog to wait at crosswalks, or just in the middle of the sidewalk while you tie your shoe. Incorporate different events into your walk to practice real-life scenarios that may come up on your walk. All the while, your dog's shoulders should be in line (or very close) with your leg.

Sometimes dogs have a really hard time walking on a leash. Pulling is a serious issue that can make walks a chore. If your dog is difficult, there are different harnesses and collars to try. If you choose a harness, pick one with the leash fastener on the front. This way, your dog is unable to pull without spinning them toward you. Avoid harnesses that clip on from the back, because this only makes it more comfortable for them to drag you down the street. Some trainers use prong collars for serious cases because it allows the dog to self-correct without injuring themselves. However, it's important to use positive training alongside any kind of self-correction methods. Choke chains can injure a dog's throat if they pull too hard and should be avoided. Ideally, the flat collar should be used on all dogs, but sometimes other measures need to be taken to keep you and your dog safe on a walk. If you have serious issues with walks, talk to a trainer to help you with your difficult dog. They may have some insight as to how you can improve your training practices.

When going on walks, remember to give frequent feedback to your dog. Let them know when they're doing a good job, and correct them when they're not doing so well. Bring lots of treats, and water for hot weather walking, when you go on your daily walks to encourage your dog to explore new places and be on their best behavior. With lots of hard work, you'll love the special time of day when you and your buddy get to enjoy some time in nature together.

If you only ever train your Goldendoodle in these five areas, you'll have a well-rounded, well-behaved dog. However, there's no reason to stop when you've mastered these few skills! Use these commands as a base and work on more advanced skills so you can keep your dog's mind active. Meanwhile, remember to practice these basics on a regular basis. Conditioning requires repetition, so by continuing to practice the same skills in different settings, you'll improve your chances of your dog acting on the first command, every time.

CHAPTER 13
Advanced Commands

O nce you've mastered the basic commands, don't stop there! Goldendoodles are known for their intelligence. When a dog gets into the routine of learning new commands, they often behave better than if they're left to their own devices. By introducing a new command on a regular basis, you can keep your dog in "work mode" until you run out of tricks to teach.

With a little more freedom in the commands you can teach once the essentials are taught, you can start adding in tricks that have no practical purpose, other than fun. However, there are still plenty of challenging, useful commands you can teach your Goldendoodle. This chapter is by no means a comprehensive list of advanced commands you can teach your Goldendoodle, but merely a few suggestions of commands you might want to try when you run out of ideas.

Leave It

This is one of those practical commands you'll use often if your Goldendoodle is curious and likes to investigate everything. Your dog may want to stick their snout into anything that looks interesting, even if it's dangerous or dirty. While it's nice to allow your dog to explore the world around you, sometimes you just know what's best for them. This command is useful if they are focused on something they shouldn't be, like a live rabbit that's teasing your dog on your daily walk, or a dead rabbit that your dog wants to pick up.

To teach this command, find a treat or a toy they love. Set it on the ground, with your foot nearby. Naturally, they're going to approach the reward so they can take it. When they get close, cover the treat with your foot so it's unavailable. Show them that they can't just eat any treat on the ground without your permission.

Try it again, asking them to leave it. If they dart toward the treat, tell them "no" and cover the treat. Repeat this until they appear uninterested or wait for the treat. If they successfully leave the treat, mark the behavior with a "yes" and give them the treat. This command should teach them to break their concentration when you tell them to "leave it." When your dog starts to get the hang of this command, you can command your

Photo Courtesy of
Stacy Borchert

dog to "leave it," then teach them to "take it." You may teach "take it" by giving them a release like "okay, take it" and making the treat or toy available to them. Now, you have opposite commands that can be useful in real-world situations, or when you're playing a game. It's a lot of fun to watch your dog override their instinct to pick up the thing they want, and it's a good practice in being obedient.

Drop It

Interesting Fact
GANA

Goldendoodles are not yet recognized by the American Kennel Club as a distinct breed, but in 2009, nonprofit organization the Goldendoodle Association of North America (GANA) was created in order to promote responsible Goldendoodle breeding and establish breed standards. Breeder members of GANA agree to a code of ethics and follow rigid health testing requirements. A registry has been established by GANA to track Goldendoodle lineage. GANA is the first and only official breed club for Goldendoodles.

"Drop it" is a command that can save your dog's life if you catch them in a potentially dangerous situation. Dogs are known to eat all kinds of non-food items. Sometimes the things they pick up are choking hazards, like a stick, or will make them sick, like a poisonous houseplant. This command will ensure that if you catch them with something they shouldn't have, they'll drop it instantly. Oftentimes, dogs know when they have a forbidden object in their possession, but don't want to give it up. Dog owners are too familiar with the ornery look in their dog's eyes before they dash away in an attempt to keep their prized possession. When practiced thoroughly, your dog will give up their prize at your command.

This command can be taught during playtime as part of a fun game. Throw a ball and have them fetch it. If your dog doesn't automatically hand it over, this is the time to teach this skill. Many dogs don't understand that your want them to drop it so you can throw the ball again. As your dog stands in front of you with the ball in their mouth, show your dog that you have a treat. They'll want to eat it, but can't because there's already a ball in their mouth. If the treat is more rewarding than the ball, they'll drop the ball in favor of the treat. When they do this, say, "good drop it" and praise them. After a few tries, start using the command when they come to you with the ball. If they drop it when you ask, give them the treat and praise, then throw the ball again for an added

Photo Courtesy of
Pam Nester

reward. Once your dog has the hang of this, move on to different objects until they drop everything on command. As your dog gets good at this, raise the stakes with objects they really don't want to drop, like a new, tasty bone, or even a treat. If your dog is willing to let go of a treat, then you should feel confident that your dog would drop a dead animal when commanded to.

Also, if your dog hasn't mastered this skill and you desperately need them to drop something they don't want to give up, use a high-value treat to persuade them. They'll likely want the treat you have in your hand and drop the forbidden object for long enough for you to grab it and quickly dispose of it. Then, you can work on conditioning your dog to drop on command.

Sit Pretty

Photo Courtesy of Sandy Hunt

There's nothing particularly useful about this trick, but it is very cute to see your Goldendoodle sitting on their hind legs like a little person. This trick is also known as "beg" but you don't need to teach the annoying persistence for treats that goes along with real begging! Along with this trick being absolutely adorable, it will help with your dog's core strength because it requires your dog to use muscles they usually don't need to engage. If your dog hasn't used these muscles a lot, then it's going to take some time to get used to sitting like a person. Your dog will probably be a little wobbly at first and you may need to give them a little support to keep them from tipping over. Keep practicing until they can hold the position.

To teach this command, have your dog start in the sitting position. Hold a treat in front of their nose, then slowly move it up and back behind their head. If they're following the treat with their nose, they'll naturally lift their body so they don't tip over backwards. Reward them if they lift off of their front paws. Keep practicing until your dog can sit on their hind legs with their paws in front of their belly. From here, play around with other fun tricks, like having your dog go from sitting to standing as they balance on their hind legs. You might even try to incorporate a shake or high five once they get really good at balancing.

Play Dead/Roll Over

Play dead/roll over is another fun trick that doesn't have much of a practical use, but is a lot of fun. However, if your dog does not like to expose their belly to people, then this is going to be a challenge. It's not natural for every dog to feel comfortable in that position. If your dog is hesitant, keep trying, but never physically force your dog to roll onto their back. This may cause them to panic because they feel as though they're being forced to submit to a bigger and stronger animal. However, Goldendoodles are usually pretty easy-going, so you probably won't have issues with this particular command.

Start with your dog in the sit position. Use the treat to guide your dog into the following positions: lower the treat to the floor to get them lying down and slowly rotate the treat around their head, until they lie on their side. Praise them and give the reward if your dog hits the desired "dead" position. For some, this is just a still dog on their side. For others, they like their dog's legs to stick straight into the air. Some owners like to make a gun with their hand and say "bang" as the command word. Others like to say "dead dog" or "play dead.". Your dog will respond to whatever cues you teach him, so feel free to get creative. Just make sure that whatever command you use is only a few syllables long and doesn't sound like another common command.

A "play dead" position is halfway to a "roll over" position. Instead of stopping the rolling motion when your dog gets to their side, continue rotating the treat for an entire roll. It may take some time until your dog is able to make a full revolution. But, when he does, make sure to give your dog a ton of praise because it's a fairly challenging trick. As your dog gets the hang of this, try to work up some speed so your dog can quickly go through the motions without much prompting. Once you master one rotation, try to get your dog to turn the other way, too.

Crawl

This is another fun and fairly simple trick that's easy to teach if your dog already knows basic commands, like "down.". This trick may also be useful to practice skills that are used in agility training. To teach this command, start with your dog in the down position. Hold the treat between their paws, then slowly move it towards you. If you move the treat too quickly, your dog will probably go back up to standing. As your dog moves towards you, you'll have to back up a little so there's enough room for your dog to move forward. If your dog crawls a foot or two without standing up, give them their reward. Keep practicing to create more distance, and then try getting them to crawl without the use of the treat.

Competitions for Goldendoodles

Your dog can compete, even if he isn't a purebred. Any dog with the right training and temperament can participate in a variety of activities for dogs. Not only can competitions boost your dog's skills and self-esteem, but it's also a great way to socialize with other dogs and humans. Plus, it's a fun way to spend lots of quality time with your dog, doing something that benefits the both of you. You'd be surprised at all of the fun things a Goldendoodle can learn how to do.

Agility training might be a lot of fun for an energetic Goldendoodle. This is basically just an obstacle course for dogs. Your dog will learn how to weave through pylons, run up and down ramps, and speed through tunnels. Focused Goldendoodles do well at agility because they're naturally driven and energetic. Goldendoodles are quick and smart, so they're capable of learning the necessary skills and carrying them out at a fast pace. Even if you don't make it to competition, there are classes where you can learn and practice the skills just for fun. It's also an awesome activity for your dog to participate in during the winter when it's harder to burn off that Goldendoodle energy.

If your dog has a knack for learning commands, obedience competitions may be your thing. These competitions require your dog to walk around a ring, sit, lie down, and stay, among other things. There are also more relaxed obedience competitions that allow you to freestyle and show off the fun tricks you've been working on with your dog. Your Goldendoodle may be especially good at these competitions because close proximity to other dogs is a challenge for some breeds, but less so for the social Goldendoodle. A smart, well-socialized, and relaxed Goldendoodle could be great at these competitions.

Nose work is another dog sport that's becoming increasingly popular because it uses your dog's strengths to their advantage. These competitions allow your dog to identify and follow scents. Your dog doesn't have to be particularly athletic to participate, either. This is a good activity for an intelligent dog with a lot of mental energy, so it's perfect for a Goldendoodle. If your dog spends all of their free time with their nose in the ground, this might be fun for your Goldendoodle.

Once you master these advanced commands, there are plenty more for you to try. April Power from Power Puppies LLC

suggests owners watch YouTube videos to learn how to teach certain commands. So, if you get an idea of something you want your Goldendoodle to do, there's a very good chance someone else has figured out how to teach the command and has filmed it! Or, if you're out of ideas, you can always do a generic search for dog tricks and choose whichever one catches your eye. Training is a fun bonding activity for you and your Goldendoodle that can continue throughout your dog's life. By giving them a "job" and lots of motivation, you can burn physical and mental energy at once, while shaping their obedience skills.

CHAPTER 14
Traveling with Goldendoodles

"Goldendoodles make awesome travel companions. They love car rides and love to tag along wherever you go."

Jewell
Jewells Puppy Paws

Goldendoodles make excellent travel companions. They generally like to go on car rides, especially if that means they get to spend some time near their favorite person. Traveling with a well-behaved dog is a pleasure because you get to do fun and exciting things alongside your best friend. However, like anything else regarding your Goldendoodle, a little preparation will make your travels with your dog so much more enjoyable.

Dog Carriers and Car Restraints

Photo Courtesy of Nitin Kayathi

Just as you would never let a child ride in your car without a seatbelt, you would never want your dog to ride unrestrained in your car. Even a crash at a relatively slow speed, or a quick stop, can send your dog flying toward the windshield. If the force of the sudden stop doesn't cause fatal injuries, it can still do a lot of harm to a dog that doesn't understand how car travel works so they can brace themselves for impact. Their anatomy makes it hard for them to sit still in normal car movement, so it's not possible for them to keep themselves safe if the car stops suddenly.

Also, it's not safe for an energetic dog to be climbing all over the car while you're driving. This presents a humongous distraction for the driver. You may think that you're skilled at driving and you can handle your best friend in the passenger seat, but it only takes a second for your dog to do something to divert your attention, like hop in your lap or lunge at your window at a passing car. Most times, this won't be a major problem, but it only takes one mistake to endanger both you and your dog.

Photo Courtesy of Vickie Robertson

For these reasons, it's imperative that you find some sort of car carrier or restraint that works best for both you and your dog. You want your Goldendoodle to be comfortable enough to enjoy car trips, but safe enough to survive the ride. There are many different options, so if one method doesn't work well, there's another that will.

A crate is probably the simplest car restraint if your Goldendoodle is crate trained. If not, it might be difficult to jam your pup into a crate if the enclosed space makes them feel nervous. But, if a crate is already your dog's safe space, they'll be at ease as you go for a ride. The rigid walls of the crate keep your dog contained, while keeping debris and other projectiles from hitting your dog in the event of a crash.

If your dog is not crate trained, or a crate doesn't fit into your car, a dog seatbelt is your next best bet. The simplest seatbelt is just a strap that connects from your car's seatbelt buckle to a clip that can be attached to your dog's collar or harness. When using a seatbelt, it's best to use a harness. In the event of an accident, the seatbelt will tug on your dog with a lot of force. If it's connected to a collar, it will pull on the neck. If it's connected to a harness, it will disperse some of the force around your dog's shoulders and chest.

You can also purchase seat dividers that will keep your dog from being thrown around the car. If your dog has been relegated to the way-back of your SUV, you can buy a divider that keeps your dog from crawling over the seats. If your dog rides in the middle, a hammock that stretches from the front headrests to the middle headrests will keep your car clean and your dog contained.

While some options for keeping your dog restrained in your car may be more effective than others, it's important that you use something to keep your Goldendoodle safe. If you'd never let a family member ride in your car without buckling up, you shouldn't let your dog do that either. When we place dogs in our world and expect them to do the same things people do, we must take extra precautions to keep them safe, as they're often not equipped with the same instincts as humans are.

Preparing Your Goldendoodle for Car Rides

For the most part, Goldendoodles will not have any issues when it comes to hopping in the car. Many will see a ride as a great opportunity to hang out in close quarters with their people. It can also be exciting to go somewhere new or see new sights from the window. However, not all dogs take to car travel so well. For some dogs, car rides can be scary. So, it's best to get your dog acclimated to the vehicle before you force them to go on a ride.

To do this, start by opening your car door and letting them explore on their own. If they choose to hop in, give them a treat and praise. If they're a little more hesitant, give them time to sniff around. When they're ready, try to lure them into the car with a treat. Most dogs will hop right in for the chance to eat a tasty snack. Then, just sit in your car with your dog, giving them lots of praise and pets.

Photo Courtesy of Madison Cruse

When your dog is comfortable with the car, it's time to take them out for a spin! At first, a short trip around the block is sufficient. Then, maybe a trip to the grocery store is good. Keep building up the time you spend in your car and reward your dog if they're calm. By the time you need to drive to the vet, your dog will be comfortable with going on rides.

You might also want to be mindful of the places you take your dog in your car. If you only go to the vet once a year, and your dog hates the vet, your dog might associate car rides with fear. So, make sure to occasionally drive your Goldendoodle some place that they love, like the dog park or a friend's house.

Car sickness is somewhat rare in dogs, but it does happen. If your dog gets queasy on car trips, the first explanation is usually anxiety. These nerves can be settled by properly acclimating your dog to the car. But some dogs are more nervous than others, so they may require a little more time and practice to feel comfortable in the car. If the fear is real, a vet may be able to prescribe anti-anxiety medications for when car travel is unavoidable.

FUN FACT
What are Emotional Support Dogs?

Emotional support dogs, also known as comfort dogs, do not receive specialized training, but, as their name implies, they provide emotional support for people with a variety of emotional and mental diagnoses including depression, PTSD, and anxiety. Dogs have been shown to increase the production of feel-good chemicals in the brain simply by interacting with humans. Emotional support dogs, comfort dogs, and therapy dogs are not recognized as service animals under the Americans with Disabilities Act, and therefore, laws regarding these animals vary widely by area.

If your pooch is totally calm in the car and still gets sick, a vet might be able to prescribe a medication that can help your carsick Goldendoodle.

When you're ready to hit the road for a long car trip, make sure to pack all of your dog's essentials. Water, food, toys, treats, collars and leashes, and identification tags are all important to have on hand. When you're on the road for a long time, make sure to make fairly frequent stops in safe places so your dog can stretch his legs. During these breaks, make sure your dog's water is available. If possible, you might want to plan a stop in a town that has a dog park so your Goldendoodle can get their daily exercise.

If you're visiting a new place, it's important to have identification on your dog. A collar tag with your name and contact info will be a lifesaver if your Goldendoodle gets lost. Also, consider having your dog microchipped. This way, if your dog becomes lost and their tag comes off, you'll still have your contact information on them if they get picked up by a rescue. It's unpleasant to think about, but it's the best chance you have if you become separated from your dog and you're far from home.

Flying and Hotel Stays

Photo Courtesy of Katina Hall

If you're going to travel long distances, you need to make extra accommodations for your Goldendoodle. If you must take a plane, it's important to take extra precautions to keep your dog calm and safe. Air travel can be nerve-wracking for both dog and human. Most likely, your dog will have to travel in the plane's cargo hold, unless you can manage to keep your Goldendoodle with you in the cabin. In the cargo hold, your dog will need to be secured in a crate. Temperatures can vary, so you might want to place a familiar blanket in the bottom. You'll also want to make food and water available if you're on a long flight. Unfortunately, dogs can become lost like other pieces of luggage, so be sure to have your contact information both on the dog and on their crate. You might also want to keep airline and airport contact information handy in case you become separated from your dog.

Air travel can be traumatizing for a dog. They'll likely be separated from you and placed somewhere loud and scary. The change in air pressure can feel strange and uncomfortable. If you're on a long flight, your dog may be wondering when he'll get to go outside next. Because of this, it may be best to travel by car, even if it is an inconvenience. Of course, if you have no other option than to travel by plane, be sure to plan ahead so your dog is comfortable and safe. You may even want to visit a vet before your trip so your dog can be deemed healthy enough to travel.

When you get to your destination, you'll likely be staying in an unfamiliar place such as a hotel, so you'll want to make it as comfortable as possible for your dog. Meanwhile, it's important to keep your dog under control, as to not be a burden to other hotel guests. No one wants to listen to a dog bark through the too-thin walls of a hotel room!

It's important to make sure your dog has plenty of exercise and attention while you're on your trip. A lonely, bored, energetic dog can do a lot of damage and annoy a lot of strangers. Make sure to give your dog their normal exercise, or maybe even a little extra. That way, you can leave your hotel knowing that your dog won't be barking and chewing on pillows while you're gone.

Never assume that your dog is welcome in any hotel, especially without notifying hotel staff. Many hotels do not allow dogs and will hand down serious fines and may force you to leave. Book a dog-friendly place in advance and pay the associated fees for your furry friend. That will help you get your vacation off to a good start. If possible, try to find a hotel that is located near a park or a walking path. Otherwise, you may have to drive or walk in unsavory areas to get to a place where you can get some exercise. As always, a little extra planning will go a long way when it comes to your dog's comfort and your sanity.

Photo Courtesy of
Jewell
Jewels Puppy Paws

Kennels and Dog Sitters

In the end, you might decide that it's best if your Goldendoodle stays home while you travel. Traveling with a dog can be fun, but it can also add a lot of stress to both you and your dog. If you know your dog will be left alone for the majority of your trip, it might be best to have them stay. In this case, a dog kennel or a dog sitter can make sure your dog is cared for while you're gone.

Kennels are great for the social Goldendoodle. If your dog loves to be around other dogs, he'll feel right at home amongst other boarders. In these facilities, there are usually a few employees on staff to make sure your dog receives the care they need, and will make sure no problems arise while socializing with other dogs. Because this is a business that watches multiple dogs at once, it can be a lot more affordable to board your dog than to hire a private sitter. Also, with someone constantly around to monitor your dog, you might feel better knowing that your dog will be well attended to.

On the other hand, not every Goldendoodle thrives in social settings, especially around a bunch of unfamiliar dogs. Some dogs are creatures

Photo Courtesy of Ira Selwin

of comfort and dislike being away from their familiar smells for too long. If this describes your dog, you might want to hire a sitter while you're away. This allows your dog to have one-on-one time with someone who attends to his basic needs. You can hire a sitter to come to your home to take care of your dog, or hire one that will care for your dog in their home. This option is usually a little more expensive, but worth it if you know your Goldendoodle wouldn't do well in a kennel.

With either option you choose, it's nice to visit with the people you're hiring to watch your Goldendoodle. If you choose a kennel, visit the facilities to make sure they're clean and the dogs are well-cared for. Chat with the employees and get a feel for their knowledge and passion for dog care. Have your dog meet with their sitter before you leave so they feel comfortable with the new person. Use this time to make sure you've made the right choice in caretaker. It's hard to relax while you're gone if you're worried about your dog's care. By properly vetting your dog's caretakers, you can ensure that your dog is in the best hands while you're away.

Traveling with your Goldendoodle should be fun and relaxing, though it's understandable why that's not always the case! Dogs love routine, and breaking that routine and familiarity may cause them to act out. First, do whatever you can to make your dog feel prepared for your trip. If that means you need to drive around town with your dog in their new crate, or leave them home alone for a few hours, then do so. During your trip, try to give your dog as much exercise and attention as possible so they can relax when you need them to be calm. Finally, use your best judgment as to what the most suitable option for your dog is. Maybe it's necessary for your dog to travel with you, or maybe it's best to hire a sitter. Keep your dog's best interests in mind, even if that means separating yourself from your best friend for a few days. Whether you're traveling to the other side of town, or the other side of the world, some preparation will ensure that everyone has a safe and happy trip.

CHAPTER 15
Grooming Your Goldendoodle

One of the reasons Goldendoodles are so popular is because of their good looks. As an owner, you want your dog to look their best at all times. At the same time, good hygiene is not just about having a pretty dog—grooming has a lot of really great health benefits. This chapter will cover all of the things you need to do to make sure your Goldendoodle looks and feels their best.

Coat Basics

"Some Poodles carry unknown shedding genes. Your breeder should be familiar with coat genetics to ensure you're going to get a mostly non-shedding Goldendoodle."

April Powers
Power Puppies LLC

There is some variation in the Goldendoodle coat. Depending on their genes, a Goldendoodle can have a straight, wavy, or curly coat, though straight-coated Goldendoodles are rare and less desirable. If you want a coat that doesn't shed much, the curlier the coat is, the better.

Even though this breed doesn't shed as much as other breeds, you'll still want to brush your Goldendoodle on a regular basis. Otherwise, the fur can become tangled and create mats. Once mats form, you'll have to remove them with scissors, which can leave unsightly bald patches on your pup. Mats can also be uncomfortable for your dog, so it's best to prevent them in the first place.

A regular wire pin brush works well for this breed, especially if they have short hair. Brush your dog a few times a week to detangle and redistribute oils throughout the coat. For many dogs, brushing feels nice, like getting a good scratch all over. But if your dog is too antsy to stay still for this part of the grooming process, you might want to wait until you've returned from a strenuous workout.

Photo Courtesy of
Maureen Simpson
Arizona Goldendoodles

Professional Grooming

"Professional grooming costs anywhere from $60-100 and they need to be groomed every 4-6 weeks and/or brushed daily if you want a longer coat."

Amie Paulson
Clovie's Creation

Goldendoodles are one of those breeds that look best when they've received a fresh haircut. Not only does the trim improve their appearance, but it helps keep long hairs out of the eyes and mouth. If you go too long without trims, your dog may have their vision partially blocked by fur, or their eyes could be irritated by hairs falling into their eyes.

According to Amie Paulson of Clovie's Creation, Goldendoodles should visit their groomer for a trim about every four to six weeks. When grooming costs between fifty and a hundred dollars a pop, this can add up quickly—that's another reason to create a budget for dog care! When you bring your dog to the groomer, you can specify what you want done with your dog's coat. Chances are, your groomer will have a lot of experience with Poodle breeds and opt for the standard cut. However, if you like your dog's fur a certain length, you can absolutely ask for a specific trim.

HELPFUL TIP
Healthy Coat, Happy Dog

Regular grooming is the key to a healthy coat for your Goldendoodle. Since Goldendoodles' fur can become easily matted, it's important to catch tangled fur before it reaches that point. Experts recommend brushing Goldendoodles at least every other day to prevent matting. An additional step that many Goldendoodle owners take is to use detangling spray while brushing their dog. This spray can help avoid matting by conditioning the fur and make the brushing experience more enjoyable for your dog. Talk to your local dog groomer or vet for detangling recommendations.

While you're at the groomer, you can have them do all of the other grooming tasks you need to have done. You may find that it's best if you hire someone else to bathe your dog and trim their toenails on a regular schedule. Some dogs do not want to sit still for their grooming, which causes a lot of stress for the owner. Groomers have a lot of experience with working with difficult dogs, if your Goldendoodle fits into that category.

However, there are some things you can do to help prepare your dog for the groomer. Make sure your dog is comfortable with other people touching him, for starters. Have a friend pet or brush your dog while you're out of the line of sight. Or, when you give your dog a bath, give them lots of praise and treats when you hit them with the water and shampoo. Practice touching your dog's toes when you're sitting on the couch, and give them praise when they don't flinch. Your groomer will thank you when your dog sits still during their appointment.

Bathing

Eventually, your Goldendoodle will locate the only mud puddle at the park or roll around in something smelly. When this happens, you'll need to give your canine buddy a bath. This is easiest if your tub has a removable shower head, though a plastic cup can help you rinse your dog in a pinch. You'll also need a shampoo specifically formulated for dogs. Because Poodles tend to have skin allergies, a gentle shampoo works well for these dogs.

To bathe your dog, give them a quick rinse and massage the shampoo into their coat. Start with

Photo Courtesy of Tracey Webster

the neck and work your way to the tail. Then rinse your dog thoroughly. When you feel as though you got all of the shampoo out, give them another rinse. Dried shampoo can irritate the skin and make your dog look dull and feel itchy. Next, take a damp rag and gently wipe your dog's face. You want to avoid pouring water directly onto your dog's face because it can get into sensitive areas and cause discomfort. Once your dog is clean, towel dry them and give them a treat for their cooperation.

Even though there's nothing better than snuggling with a freshly washed dog, try to limit how often you shampoo your dog. Too much washing can dry out your dog's skin and coat, causing them to feel uncomfortable. One bath every three to four months is a good goal, with extra baths if your dog is especially dirty or stinky.

Trimming Nails

Trimming your dog's nails in an important task. Not only do you want to keep your dog's claws from tearing up your furniture and skin, but overgrown nails can cause health problems for your dog. If dogs walk on long claws for too long, it puts unnecessary stress on their paws. Over time, this can create a lot of pain and discomfort for your dog. If you can hear clicking and scraping when you walk your dog on concrete, that's a good indicator that your dog's nails need a trim.

This is something you can do at home with a pair of dog nail clippers. These can be purchased at any pet store. Simply hold the opening of the clippers around the end of your dog's toenail and squeeze until the metal goes through the nail. As long as you don't cut through the quick, or the blood supply, your dog shouldn't feel any pain. If your Goldendoodle has clear nails, the quick is easy to see—it's the pink part of the nail. If your pup has dark nails, it's a little more difficult to distinguish. If you're worried about cutting the quick, you can ask a vet to show you where to cut the next time you go in for a checkup. But, if you're only taking the sharp ends off in small snips, you probably don't need to worry about injuring your dog.

Many dogs hate the sensation of having their nails trimmed. For this reason, it's important to train your dog to handle nail trimmings at a young age. To start, just touch your dog's paws and nails. If they allow this, give them a treat and praise. Next, introduce the clipper and hold it near their toes. If they stay calm, give them a treat. Gradually increase the proximity until your dog sits still as you clip a toenail. If they allow this, give them a good treat and lots of praise. Repeat this until they connect nail trimming with good treats.

Brushing Teeth

This is another grooming task that is important for your dog's overall health. Tooth decay can cause serious problems for your dog, including painful chewing and even heart disease. Having your dog's teeth professionally cleaned can be expensive and requires your dog to go under anesthesia, which can be hard on some dogs' bodies. To avoid these issues later in life, regular brushing is necessary.

First, purchase toothpaste from a pet store in a flavor your dog will enjoy. Never use human toothpaste on a dog, because they're not able to spit out the foam like people can. Next, choose a brush that fits your dog's teeth. Some owners like to use a traditional handled toothbrush, while others like to use a little scrubber that fits on your fingertip. Some even use a child's toothbrush. Use whichever is most comfortable for you and your dog.

After applying paste to the brush, let your dog give it a lick. This will introduce them to the flavor of the paste and will reduce the surprise of you sticking a strange object in their mouth. Gently pull back their lips and start brushing. Focus on the outsides of the teeth, as this is the dirtiest part of the tooth. Brush into their gum line, but not so vigorously that you cause bleeding. It can be tricky to get all of the teeth covered, but you'll eventually work out a system for gaining access to every pearly white. When you're finished, give your dog lots of praise for their cooperation. Repeat this process several times a week to keep plaque at bay, or make it a part of your daily routine.

Cleaning Ears and Eyes

Goldendoodles have floppy ears that can become infected if too much moisture is trapped inside. Because of this, you'll have to pay special attention to the cleanliness of your pup's ears. Itchiness and redness are good signs that something is amiss. If the problem persists and you can tell your dog is very uncomfortable, take him into the vet for a checkup. Your vet will be able to diagnose and treat a possible infection.

To prevent ear problems, make sure to keep your dog's ears dry. In the bath, take special care to avoid splashing water in your dog's face. If your dog loves to swim, give the flaps of your dog's ears a pat with a towel or a cotton ball. If your dog develops a waxy buildup or is especially itchy, give their ears a rinse with ear cleaning fluid. This can be purchased at a vet's office or pet store. Squirt a little fluid into the ear canal and massage the base of the ear to work in the product. Your dog will shake their head, dislodging the buildup. You may even wet the corner of a washcloth with the solution and wipe down the outer parts of the ear. However, it's important to avoid the inner ear. Never touch the part of the ear that can't easily be wiped with a washcloth. Even if your dog's ear looks dirty and you think you're careful, placing Q-tips or other small implements into the ear canal can cause a lot of damage. If you feel as though the problem has persisted after your cleaning, it's time to go to the vet.

You should also take care when cleaning the area around your dog's eyes. Regular trims can keep your dog's eyes clear of scratchy, overgrown fur. If your dog accumulates gunk around the corners of their eyes, gently wipe it away with a damp cloth. Try not to pick at the area around their eyes, because it only takes one wrong move to poke your pooch in the eye. If your Goldendoodle has a light coat and their tears cause staining, there are products that can help. While a little gunk around the eyes is normal, excessive discharge can be a sign of a more serious problem. If your dog's eyes appear especially red, watery, or gooey, a visit to your vet is in order.

Home Grooming vs. Professional Grooming

Photo Courtesy of Sara Hester

Now that you've been introduced to all of the regular grooming your Goldendoodle requires, you'll have to decide which tasks you can handle at home, and which are best left to the professionals. As long as the care you're giving doesn't require a veterinary professional, like treating infections or scaling teeth, you can do all of your grooming at home. If you're on a budget, the more you can do yourself, the better it is for your wallet.

On the other hand, not all dogs tolerate grooming well. If your dog gives you a hard time every time you try to touch his nails, you might decide that it's best to leave that to a groomer, who has lots of experience dealing with sensitive dogs. Sometimes dogs tolerate grooming if it's not their owner doing the work. And, unless you're careful with sharp scissors, you can cause a lot of harm. Besides, an experienced groomer has perfected the Goldendoodle cut. If you aren't as skilled with the scissors, your poor dog may end up looking silly. There's a good reason that dog groomers exist in virtually every pet store and vet office!

Perhaps the best rule of thumb is to do whatever you're comfortable doing, and defer the rest to a pro. Maybe you're comfortable with brushing the coat and the teeth, but everything else makes you nervous to do on your own. Or, maybe you're fine to bathe your dog, but you need someone with a little artistic vision to control the clippers. Or, maybe your Goldendoodle loves their time at the doggy spa, and you love not

having to wrestle with your dog to get them in your tub. As long as your dog's hygiene needs are met, it doesn't matter who does them!

Goldendoodles are medium-maintenance dogs when it comes to grooming, so expect to put some time and money into keeping them clean. A well-groomed dog not only looks and smells nice, but may feel healthier, too. When acclimating your dog to anything new, remember to start slow and give lots of treats and encouragement. With the right conditioning, your dog will learn to tolerate grooming, and even enjoy the time you spend keeping your dog looking sharp. If your dog's grooming ever requires more expertise than you think you possess, you can always hire a groomer to do some of the services beyond your talents. In the end, you just want your Goldendoodle to look and feel his very best.

CHAPTER 16
Nutrition and Healthcare

There is nothing more important than the good health of your Goldendoodle. Our pets instantly become valued members of our families, and good owners will do whatever it takes for their dogs to stay happy and healthy. Exercise, good hygiene, and proper training go a long way toward keeping your dog in good shape, but proper nutrition and the right healthcare really round out your dog's overall good health. You may feel as though there's a lot of pressure on you to keep your best friend healthy, but it's simpler than you may think. If you know the basics of good nutrition and healthcare, then you can rely on the professionals for situations that need more expertise.

The Importance of a Good Diet

Your Goldendoodle is basically a ball of energy. An active mind controls an energetic body that will go for hours. Your dog's motor needs the right kind of fuel to keep them moving, while replenishing their bodies. A lack of nutrition will leave you with a dog that is dull and fatigued. Proper nutrition will help keep your dog's brain in top condition, their coat soft and glossy, and their muscles strong. A diet full of the right balance of nutrients rather than a diet full of junk may even make a difference in your dog's longevity.

Just because it appears as though dogs can eat anything, it doesn't mean that they should. Dogs need a certain mix of nutrients that comes from a good dog food. The bulk of these foods is usually carbohydrates. These give your dog the fuel they need to run and play. Simple carbohydrates, like sugar, are burned quickly for fast energy. Complex carbs, like whole grains, take longer to break down. This gives your dog longer-lasting energy to keep them energized between meals. When looking for dog foods, search for ingredients like brown rice, oatmeal, or sweet potatoes. These are all nutrient-dense carbs.

When it comes to your dog's protein intake, look for a food that has around 30% protein. Canines are meat eaters, so a food that skimps on the meat will deprive your dog of the amino acids they need to maintain healthy muscles and blood. Foods that have a variety of meats allow your dog to have a good mix of beneficial nutrients. For example, red meats like beef are packed with iron. Chicken is a lean source of protein, and its cartilage is great for your dog's joints. Fish is another lean source of protein and contains omega fatty acids that do wonders for your dog's skin, coat, and brain. Though all of these meat sources are good, the meat your dog eats will probably come down to their personal preference. Some Goldendoodles will eat anything in their dish, while others demand a certain flavor of food.

Fats are a vital part of a dog's diet that should not be omitted. Fats keep your dog's coat smooth, provide lots of energy, and help your dog absorb vitamins. Fats in dog food come from meat sources, vegetable oils, and fish oil. It may make you feel squeamish to see ingredients like chicken meal, beef fat, or cartilage in your dog's food, but these are all nutritious parts of the animal that your dog needs in their diet.

Many well-meaning dog owners feed their dogs diets that don't fit the nutritional needs of canines. Occasionally, a dog owner will feed their dog according to trends in human diets, a completely different species with different needs. For example, carbs are the most recent nutrient to become vilified. In the past, fats were seen as a nutrient to avoid. However, both are vital to a dog's longevity. Or, a vegan human might decide that their dog should live on fruits and leafy greens alone. If you have concerns about your dog's nutrition, it's best to consult with a veterinarian before putting your dog on a fad diet.

How to Choose a Dog Food

"We have found that many seem to be sensitive to chicken, even if it doesn't appear on allergy tests."

Tamara Spridgeon
Daizy Doodles

Even when you know what nutrients your dog needs, it's still over-whelming to choose a food when there are so many brands and flavors to pick from. If you bought your puppy from a breeder, they probably have a preferred food they use for their dogs. Your pup will probably be used to this food, too, so you may not want to change brands. Once your puppy is an adult, you can switch from the puppy formula to the corresponding adult formula.

If you adopted a Goldendoodle, or if your pup's current food isn't working for you two, you'll have to choose from the giant wall of dog food at the pet store. First, you'll need to choose between a dry food and a wet food. If your Goldendoodle has an eating issue, then you might need a wet food. Otherwise, dry food is best for most dogs. When your dog chews dry food, the crunchy surface scrapes away at plaque on their teeth. When your dog eats a wet food, not only do they miss out on this scraping, but the wet food sticks on the teeth. So, unless your dog has an issue with chewing, or is especially picky, a dry food is typically better than a moist food.

For the most part, all commercial dog foods will contain the essential nutrients your dog needs to thrive. These foods will contain carbs, protein, fats, and a mix of vitamins and minerals, in varying amounts. Some dog foods are cheap because the ingredients they use are inexpensive. On the other hand, some dog foods are practically unaffordable because they use pricier ingredients. For this reason, it may be best to choose a dog food that's somewhere in the middle of the two extremes. That way, you'll get quality ingredients without overpaying for a brand name. From there, you'll want to choose a flavor that your dog will enjoy. Some dog food companies and pet stores will even give out samples if you're really unsure. If you try one food and your dog doesn't touch it, maybe he'll wolf down another flavor. Once you find a food that works, stick with it. While people like variety in flavors, a dog does better with consistency in their diet. Otherwise, they may develop digestive issues.

Some dog owners would prefer to feed their Goldendoodles a diet of human-grade, fresh foods, as opposed to commercial dog food. While this is fine, it's best to do so under the supervision of a veterinarian. It's more expensive and takes a lot more planning to feed your dog fresh foods, but as long as your dog gets the right nutrition, it's perfectly acceptable. Many homemade dog food recipes include proteins like chicken breast and beef organs, fats like fish oil, and carbs like rice and potatoes. Plenty of fruits and vegetables in this kind of diet will provide the vitamins and minerals your dog needs to be healthy. It takes a lot of knowledge and planning to feed your dog homemade food, but with proper supervision, it's a valid form of pet nutrition.

HELPFUL TIP
Dog Treat Bakeries

Dog treat bakeries are a sweet way to give your dog a decadent treat for a birthday, special occasion, or just an extra reward. Bakeries for dog treats are regulated by the FDA, just as human bakeries are. According to their website, "[the FDA] requires that pet foods, like human foods, be pure and wholesome, safe to eat, produced under sanitary conditions, contain no harmful substances, and be truthfully labeled." For specific regulations in your state, visit the Association of American Feed Control Officials (AAFCO).

People Food

Apart from homemade diets, dog owners have a hard time resisting giving their dog human foods. Whether you're trying to eliminate food waste in your home, or you just want to make your little buddy very happy, it's hard not to let your dog clean your plate. People food can provide excellent nutrition and superior motivation for your dog, but they can also bring on annoying behaviors and health issues. When feeding your dog from your fridge, it's important to be mindful of what exactly you're giving your pooch.

For starters, giving your dog treats from your table or plate will enforce the idea that your dog should beg. It may be cute the first few times, but it won't be when your family or guests can't sit down for a meal without your dog pawing at their leg or jumping up at the table to steal a bite. Once you teach a dog that they can have food from your plate, it's difficult to break that bad habit.

Secondly, table scraps are not always best for your dog. A lot of times, people will feed gristle from their steak or leftovers that have been prepared with dog-unfriendly ingredients like onions, chocolate, and avocados. This extra food can add to their daily calorie count and will pack on pounds over time. Even foods that aren't downright dangerous could give your dog tummy troubles. For example, some dogs may have a hard time digesting dairy, and could end up leaving a mess on your carpet if they have too much cheese.

There are some acceptable reasons for feeding your dog people food. The foods we eat may be very appetizing to your dog, making them excellent training treats. And many fruits and vegetables are low in calories and provide excellent nutrition. So, if you give your dog a little morsel of fish as a high-stakes training treat, or plop a few blueberries into their bowl, you probably won't cause any annoying behaviors or make your dog ill.

Weight Management

Because Goldendoodles are so active, their daily exercise will probably be enough to keep them from getting chunky. But it is possible for any dog to become overweight if they don't have the right balance of calories and exercise. When a dog is at their ideal weight, there should be a clear tuck in their waist around their hips, but no ribs should be visible. You want to be able to feel your dog's bones, but not see them.

As long as you follow the feeding directions on your dog food packaging, ensure your dog has a few hours of exercise a day, and you don't overdo it on the treats, you shouldn't have to worry too much about weight gain.

However, if your Goldendoodle has sudden, unexplained weight changes, see a vet immediately. If your dog is gaining weight and there's no underlying medical reason, there are some things you can do to get your dog back in shape. First, be mindful of the extras your dog gets to eat throughout the day. Do you give your dog table scraps or lots of high-calorie treats? Also, look at your dog's eating habits. If they eat most of their food at meal times, but not all of it, don't let them graze throughout the day. Instead, remove the extra food and give your dog an equal portion at their next meal. Then, work on increasing the amount of exercise your dog gets. Start slowly and work your way up until you're able to go on a few long walks a day without your pooch getting winded. If that doesn't work, cut back on their daily food allotment just a little at a time until you find the right calorie count for their activity level. Once you make the necessary adjustments to your dog's diet and exercise, they should gradually return to a healthier weight. Pudgy dogs can be cute, but the excess fat that puts strain on their body is not.

Veterinary Checkups

For your Goldendoodle's health, it's best to prevent any issues before they cause serious issues for your dog. One way to do this is to take your dog to the vet for a yearly checkup. During these regular checkups, your vet will ask you if you've noticed any changes in your dog's health or ask if you have any concerns about your Goldendoodle. Even if your concerns turn out to be nothing, it's still a good time to ask any questions you might have.

Your vet will do a quick, but thorough examination of your dog. They'll check the eyes, ears, and mouth for any abnormalities. They'll listen to your dog's heart, lungs, and belly to make sure everything sounds normal. Your dog will have their temperature taken to check for any infection. Finally, the vet will run their hands along your dog to make sure everything is fine with their legs, back, and belly.

The reason it's so important to go every year is that a vet can quickly diagnose an issue you might not even notice. And, if you go regularly, they can track changes from year to year, pinpointing issues to keep an eye on. If you only go to the vet when your dog is sick, there's no benchmark to compare to your dog's current state.

If your dog gets nervous at the vet, it might help to prepare them for what's to come. Practice looking in your dog's ears, pulling back their lips to expose their teeth, and sitting still while feeling a heartbeat. It's also helpful if a friend does these things so your dog gets used to strangers touching them. Treats will also show your dog that the vet isn't so bad. You can bring your dog's favorites to go along with the ones the vet provides.

Fleas, Ticks, and Worms

"There are specific genetic diseases that are concerns in either Golden Retrievers or Poodles but there are very few that overlap which is another good trait of Goldendoodles. We test for Von Wildebrands bleeding disorder because it is very common in poodles and possibly found in retrievers. We also test for Degenerative Myelopathy because it is found in almost all breeds of dog. The overall genetic health is much better in Doodles than it is in their ancestors because the recessive traits that have been bred into the purebred animals are negated by the low likelihood that they exist in both breeds."

Kristine Probst
Island Grove Pet Kennels

Part of preventative care is taking precautions to keep parasites off of your dog. Dogs are like magnets for these pests because they eat things they shouldn't and wander around areas with lots of vegetation. And, once the parasites latch on, it may be hard to tell that your dog has an infestation.

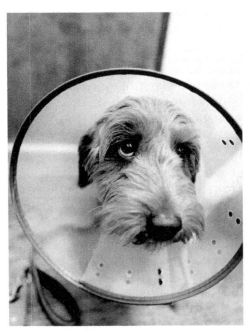

Intestinal worms are fairly common in puppies. If you notice your dog's eating habits have changed, their bowel movements are irregular, or if they're lethargic or vomiting, it's a good idea to have a vet check them out. A stool sample can quickly reveal if there are any worms in their gut and medicine can be prescribed to take care of the issue. Heartworms are another parasite that travels through the bloodstream. Infected mosquitoes bite your dog, which releases the heartworm into the bloodstream, eventually making its way to the heart. This parasite can be deadly if not treated immediately. Luckily, there's a monthly preventative medicine that can keep your dog protected against heartworms. After a quick blood test, your vet will prescribe a medication to give to your dog at the same time every month. As long as you give this medicine to your dog on a regular basis, you won't have to worry about heartworm.

Fleas and ticks are another parasite that can easily latch onto your dog. These creatures suck the blood from your dog and can possibly pass on dangerous diseases. Plus, fleas cause extreme itchiness and are hard to kill once an infestation starts. Some dogs are even allergic to flea bites, compounding on that itchiness. To prevent your dog from bringing these pests home, choose a preventative that works best for your pup. Topical preventatives can be applied to your dog's coat once a month. Or there are oral preventatives that cause fleas and ticks to die when they bite your dog. If fleas and ticks cannot survive on your Goldendoodle, then there's less of a chance of these pests reproducing and causing your dog harm.

Vaccinations

Vaccinations are another big part of preventative care and some are even required by law. There are a handful of contagious diseases that veterinarians can vaccinate against, starting when your dog is a puppy. In many places, your dog must be up to date on their recommended vaccinations in order to take training classes or go to dog parks. In fact, it's best to wait to visit dog parks until your puppy has received all of their shots. The rabies vaccine is required to license your dog because an unvaccinated dog can become a public health risk.

While vaccinations have become a hot topic in recent years, there is no reason not to vaccinate your dog. By keeping your dog free of contagious disease, you're doing your part in eliminating terrible viruses that kill lots of dogs. You're not only protecting your dog but other dogs who might not be up to date on their vaccines. When your puppy gets their first shots, your vet will put your dog on a vaccination schedule. The clinic will then notify you every time your dog needs to get booster shots to maintain their immunity. That way, you don't have to worry about your dog getting the right shots at the right time.

Genetic Illnesses

Because the Goldendoodle is half Golden Retriever and half Poodle, common genetic ailments come from both breeds. The good thing about crossbreeds is that they're less likely to suffer from deadly genetic diseases because there's less in-breeding between dogs. Also, if you're buying from a reputable breeder, their practices limit the number of genetic ailments by choosing only healthy dogs to breed with. However, there are some ailments that are more common in certain breeds, so it's a good idea to know what to look for.

There are a few conditions of the skeletal system that you'll want to look out for if your dog suddenly begins limping. Luxating patella is a condition where the kneecap slides around and "catches" in certain circumstances. The simple act of running and jumping can cause the knee to slide out of place, which can be extremely painful. Hip dysplasia is another condition that's generally found in larger breeds where the hip joint doesn't fit in the socket very well, causing pain and issues with mobility. Both conditions need to be treated with surgery if serious enough. This is common in Golden Retrievers because they grow so quickly, so it may be an issue in Goldendoodles as well.

This breed is also more likely to suffer from retinal atrophy and other eye issues. This is an eye condition that can lead to blindness over time. Of course, this is one of those conditions that should be eliminated in the breeding process. However, if you adopt a dog from an unknown origin, you may want to have your dog's eyes tested if they have trouble seeing in the dark. This is a sign that their overall eyesight is deteriorating. Poodle crossbreeds are also at a higher risk for thyroid issues. Talk to your vet if your dog is suddenly lethargic or has patchy fur. They can prescribe medications that can return their hormone levels to normal in no time.

Poodles also tend to have allergies and intolerances, both skin and gastrointestinal. Foods, plants, or other environmental factors can cause your Goldendoodle to have itchy skin. When itchy skin is left unchecked, sores and hot spots can develop on the skin. When the skin is broken, it makes it easy for bacteria to enter and cause infection. If your dog is excessively itchy, try an anti-itch spray or cream from your vet or pet store. This may provide enough relief to keep your dog from scratching. If this doesn't work, a veterinarian may prescribe medication to help stop the allergic reaction.

Poodle crossbreeds also tend to have sensitive stomachs. According to Dede Hard of Red Cedar Farms, Goldendoodles often have tender tummies and suffer from stress-related diarrhea, especially as puppies.

Photo Courtesy of Nick Frega

If you think your dog is having a reaction to their food, try a different kind and see if the gastrointestinal symptoms subside. For some dogs, it may be the chicken that doesn't agree with them. For others, it could be an issue with the grains. However, seriously consider not putting your dog on a "grain-free" food if they haven't had prior issues with certain ingredients. Recent studies have shown a link between grain-free dog foods and heart disease. Grain-free might be a current fad in dog food, but check with a vet before switching to a new formula.

Senior Dog Care

Goldendoodles have a fairly long lifespan of ten to fourteen years, but before you know it, your dog will be considered a senior dog. Senior dogs still love to play and explore, but they will slow down a little, especially compared to the energy levels they showed as a pup.

You may find that your senior dog has joint pain when they try to walk or play. This is often noticeable when they get up first thing in the morning or try to walk around after a nap. There are a few things you can do to ease this stiffness and pain. For starters, make sure that your dog has a soft and supportive bed to rest on. If they're used to hopping up on the couch, they may have a harder time doing that as they age. There are joint supplements you can give your dog that will help repair some of the damage that occurs to leg joints over time. If your dog seems to be in a considerable amount of pain, talk to your vet about anti-inflammatory medication. This may be a good remedy for joint pain.

Your older Goldendoodle may also gain weight if they're not exercising as much as they used to. Older dogs require fewer calories than their younger counterparts. If your senior dog is gaining weight, consider reducing their daily food intake. If they have trouble eating crunchy kibble due to reduced smell or painful teeth, try mixing dry and wet food together to make it easier to chew. Or, pour a little water or broth on top of the crunchy food.

You may also have to change your exercise routine. While you may have been able to go on runs before, you will reach a time where that's just too much exertion for your old dog. Exercise is still important, but you may decide that an easy walk will lead to less pain and stiffness in your dog's legs. Continuing to test your dog's mental fitness with puzzles and other games is still important as they get older. It can keep their mind sharp, which will lead to less confusion and agitation.

Most of all, it's important to spend quality time with your Goldendoodle. These dogs are companion animals and want to snuggle up to you. You may find that as your Goldendoodle ages, he's less interested in playing fetch and more interested in nestling up to you while you read a book. Cherish these moments with your dog because they won't last forever. Also, remember that dogs are considered "senior" around age eight. With proper care, it's entirely possible for your dog to live another decade as a senior dog.

Eventually, there will come a time when you have to say goodbye. If your dog is in a lot of pain, can no longer use the bathroom on their own, or is suffering from a lot of different age-related ailments, you may decide that euthanasia is the best option. This can be extremely difficult to decide for your pet, but you'll know when your dog's condition will only get worse and their quality of life is suffering. When you're reaching this conclusion, talk to a vet for guidance. An examination can tell you if there's anything they can do for your dog. If not, they will take you through the euthanasia process.

With a good diet and preventative care, your Goldendoodle will live a long and healthy life. When it comes to their diet, don't overthink it—dogs need a balanced diet with carbohydrates, protein, fats, vitamins, and minerals. They also need to burn as many calories as they eat so they can stay in a healthy size range. For veterinary care, prevention is key. Keep up on shots, use parasite preventatives, and see your vet annually to give your dog the best chance at staying healthy. And, if you're ever concerned about your Goldendoodle's health, you can always call your veterinarian.

Having a Goldendoodle is such a joy. These sweet, bubbly dogs will make sure you never have a dull day in your life. They are bright and eager to learn, but also sensitive and relaxed. Once you bring your new Goldendoodle home, you'll understand why these adorable dogs are all the rage. It takes a lot of time, energy, patience, and money to raise a dog from puppy to senior, but it's absolutely worth it. Remember, there are tons of resources available to help you understand your Goldendoodle, and they're all happy to help an owner and their dog build a solid relationship. Before you know it, you'll wonder how you ever managed to live without your furry family member!

Made in the USA
Monee, IL
07 May 2021